PATHWAYS OF TRUST
101 Shortcuts to Holiness

JOHN H. HAMPSCH, C.M.F.

SERVANT
BOOKS

PUBLISHED BY ST. ANTHONY MESSENGER PRESS
CINCINNATI, OHIO

Library of Congress Cataloging-in-Publication Data

Hampsch, John H.
 Pathways of trust : 101 shortcuts to holiness / by John H. Hampsch.
       p. cm.
 ISBN 0-86716-603-7 (alk. paper)

 1. Trust–Religious aspects–Christianity. 2. Holiness–Christianity. I.Title.
 BV4597.53.T78H36 2004
 234'.8–dc22

                                                              2004008318

Cover design and photo by Steve Eames
Book design by Mark Sullivan
ISBN 0-86716-603-7

Copyright 2004 by John H. Hampsch. All rights reserved.
Published by Servant Books, an imprint of St. Anthony Messenger Press
www.AmericanCatholic.org
Printed in the United States of America.

TABLE OF CONTENTS

ONE: *Foreword: Holiness and Trust* 1

TWO: *Spiritual Warfare and Trust* 3

THREE: *Detachment and Trust* 4

FOUR: *Faith and Trust* 5

FIVE: *Hope and Trust* 7

SIX: *Love and Trust* 9

SEVEN: *Suffering and Trust* 11

EIGHT: *Adversity and Trust* 12

NINE: *Trials and Trust* 13

TEN: *Tribulations and Trust* 14

ELEVEN: *Problems and Trust* 15

TWELVE: *Pressure and Trust* 17

THIRTEEN: *Persecution and Trust* 18

FOURTEEN: *Fear and Trust* 21

FIFTEEN: *Worry and Trust* 23

SIXTEEN: *Anxiety and Trust* 24

SEVENTEEN: *Belief and Trust* 27

EIGHTEEN: *Temptation and Trust* 28

NINETEEN: *Self-Deception and Trust* 29

TWENTY: *Self-Discipline and Trust* 30

TWENTY-ONE: *Self-Sufficiency and Trust* 32

TWENTY-TWO: *Self-Abandonment and Trust* 32

TWENTY-THREE: *Mediocrity and Trust* 34

TWENTY-FOUR: *Prosperity and Trust* 35

TWENTY-FIVE: *Inadequacy and Trust* 36

TWENTY-SIX: Obedience and Trust 37

TWENTY-SEVEN: *Acquiescence and Trust* 38

TWENTY-EIGHT: *Commitment and Trust* 39

TWENTY-NINE: *Dependence and Trust* 40

THIRTY: *Influence and Trust* 41

THIRTY-ONE: *Trustworthiness and Trust* 43

THIRTY-TWO: *Crises and Trust* 45

THIRTY-THREE: *Godliness and Trust* 46

THIRTY-FOUR: *God-Focus and Trust* 47

THIRTY-FIVE: *Endeavors and Trust* 48

THIRTY-SIX: *Persistence and Trust* 49

THIRTY-SEVEN: *Perseverance and Trust* 50

THIRTY-EIGHT: *Endurance and Trust* 51

THIRTY-NINE: *Guidance and Trust* 52

FORTY: *Prayer and Trust* 54

FORTY-ONE: *Striving and Trust* 55

FORTY-TWO: *Reliability and Trust* 57

FORTY-THREE: *Humility and Trust* 58

FORTY-FOUR: *Petition and Trust* 59

FORTY-FIVE: *Gratitude and Trust* 60

FORTY-SIX: *Discouragement and Trust* 61

FORTY-SEVEN: *Instability and Trust* 63

FORTY-EIGHT: *Charity and Trust* 64

FORTY-NINE: *Rewards and Trust* 66

FIFTY: *Optimism and Trust* 68

FIFTY-ONE: *Acceptance and Trust* 68

FIFTY-TWO: *Strength and Trust* 70

FIFTY-THREE: *Serenity and Trust* 71

FIFTY-FOUR: *Problems and Trust* 72

FIFTY-FIVE: *Fear and Trust* 73

FIFTY-SIX: *Depression and Trust* 74

FIFTY-SEVEN: *Sickness and Trust* 76

FIFTY-EIGHT: *Bereavement and Trust* 77

FIFTY-NINE: *Prudence and Trust* 79

SIXTY: *Justice and Trust* 81

SIXTY-ONE: *Long-Suffering and Trust* 83

SIXTY-TWO: *Temperance and Trust* 85

SIXTY-THREE: *Wisdom and Trust* 86

SIXTY-FOUR: *Understanding and Trust* 87

SIXTY-FIVE: *Knowledge and Trust* 89

SIXTY-SIX: *Counsel and Trust* 91

SIXTY-SEVEN: *Piety and Trust* 93

SIXTY-EIGHT: *Fortitude and Trust* 94

SIXTY-NINE: *Fear of the Lord and Trust* 95

SEVENTY: *Peace and Trust* 96

SEVENTY-ONE: *Peacefulness and Trust* 97

SEVENTY-TWO: Possessions and Trust 98

SEVENTY-THREE: *Happiness and Trust* 99

SEVENTY-FOUR: *Expectancy and Trust* 100

SEVENTY-FIVE: *Frugality and Trust* 101

SEVENTY-SIX: *Timeliness and Trust* 103

SEVENTY-SEVEN: *Contemplation and Trust* 104

SEVENTY-EIGHT: *Guilt and Trust* 105

SEVENTY-NINE: *Repentance and Trust* 107

EIGHTY: *Scripture and Trust* 109

EIGHTY-ONE: *Salvation and Trust* 111

EIGHTY-TWO: *Self-Worth and Trust* 112

EIGHTY-THREE: *Fulfillment and Trust* 113

EIGHTY-FOUR: *Encouragement and Trust* 115

EIGHTY-FIVE: *Yearning and Trust* 116

EIGHTY-SIX: *Joy and Trust* 118

EIGHTY-SEVEN: *Kindness and Trust* 119

EIGHTY-EIGHT: *Gentleness and Trust* 120

EIGHTY-NINE: *Faithfulness and Trust* 122

NINETY: *Goodness and Trust* 122

NINETY-ONE: *Weakness and Trust* 124

NINETY-TWO: *Delay and Trust* 126

NINETY-THREE: *Confidence and Trust* 129

NINETY-FOUR: *Self-Confidence and Trust* 130

NINETY-FIVE: *Self-Esteem and Trust* 131

NINETY-SIX: *Insecurity and Trust* 133

NINETY-SEVEN: *God-Sovereignty and Trust* 134

NINETY-EIGHT: *Fruitfulness and Trust* 136

NINETY-NINE: *Progress and Trust* 137

ONE HUNDRED: *Direction and Trust* 139

ONE HUNDRED ONE: *Disappointment and Trust* 140

ONE

Foreword: Holiness and Trust

Why is it easier to love your pet dog than to love a cockroach skittering across the floor? It's all a matter of relating. Call your dog to your side, and with happily wagging tail Fido will eagerly approach you, always ready to enjoy your friendly petting. The cockroach, on the other hand, is neither approaching nor approachable.

The dog and the cockroach have several things in common, however. First, they both regard you as a living reality, although one regards you as a safe person and the other as a threatening person. Second, they both have a sense of expectancy in relating to you, although one by way of goodwill, the other by way of fear. Third, they both have an implicit awareness of your power, although one is aware of your power to please, the other of your power to harm. The three qualities or terms of interaction are all positive in the dog but negative in the cockroach. The result is that the dog relates to you by way of trust, the cockroach by way of distrust.

Notice that the presence or absence of trust is equated with the presence or absence of love in the human to animal relationship. (Hence the proverbial encomium of a dog as "man's best friend.") The dog is lovable because it is trusting of a kindly master. Why does the dog trust? Essentially it is because it perceives its master as benevolent—a *benevolent person with benevolent power*, expressed in *benevolent action*. That is to say, the dog makes it easy for the master to love him, reciprocally, because he perceives the master as a loving *person* who manifests his love-activated *power* in loving *action*.

The analogy is evident when the topic of study is our spiritual life. Loving God as our divine Master is the quintessence of the spiritual life—that is, holiness. It has as its prerequisites that by our faith we accept God as a benevolent (loving and lovable) person with benevolent (love-activated) power,

1

expressed in benevolent action (his loving providence as it relates to us). The immediate outcropping of this trilogy in its fullest expression is *trust*. Trust in God is not the essence of holiness; love is the essence of holiness (see 1 Jn 4:16). Yet the trust that results from our love for God is the criterion for our holiness, and the ultimate sign of its authenticity. The more we love, the more we trust, and conversely, the more we trust, the more we love. This holds true in all of our relationships with God—even when he is disappointed in us.

Recently I saw a man throw a stick at his neighbor's dog to stop him from messing up the flowerbed. Yet the man's heart melted when the dog gleefully picked up the stick in his mouth and, with wagging tail, brought it back to the man, dropping it at his feet, where he eagerly and playfully waited for the next throw of the stick. The dog's trust, in its naiveté, was undisturbed by the man's displeasure—so much so, in fact, that it dispelled that displeasure. In the face of God's displeasure when our pursuit of holiness is retarded by sin, our trust in him and his merciful love dissolves his wrath, as the dog's trust melted the annoyance of the man in the garden. With this, the Lord accepts us again into his warm and loving friendship, assuring us that our faltering holiness has been restored, for "the law of the LORD is perfect, reviving the soul" (Ps 19:7).

Just as love has many forms of expression, including consideration, gift giving, hugging, kissing, and so on, so also is trust multifaceted in its manifestations. In this book I have attempted to delineate 101 ways of practicing trust in God. God's generosity is reminiscent of the ice cream stores that feature a wide variety of ice cream. The variegations of the virtue of trust are just another of the many ways that God's goodness is reflected. They provide us with a multitude of ways to grow in holiness—a variety of paths that lead to union with our Creator. They are some of the many graces he has promised to bestow on us to help us enjoy a superabundant spiritual life (see Jn 10:10). Let us enjoy them with zest!

TWO

Spiritual Warfare and Trust

In coping with the forces of hell in what is called spiritual warfare, a certain kind of courage or fearlessness can be reckless, rash, and irresponsible. Its opposite is an appropriate and prudent fear. Jesus incisively advocates a *prudent* fear of the evil one and his machinations, as distinguished from fear of a temporal threat: "I tell you, my friends, do not fear those who kill the body, and after that can do nothing more. But I will warn you whom to fear: fear him who, after he has killed, has authority to cast into hell. Yes, I tell you, fear him!" (Lk 12:4-5).

In the next few sentences, however, Jesus tells us how to prevent an unwarranted fear in resisting the devil, namely *by exercising a profound trust* in the Lord who cares for each of us lovingly: "Are not five sparrows sold for two pennies? Yet not one of them is forgotten in God's sight. But even the hairs of your head are all counted. *Do not be afraid*; you are of more value than many sparrows" (Lk 12:6-7, emphasis mine). Thus, paradoxically, fear and courage can work together through a combination of fear of evil and a secure courage in trusting in the Lord's protection from that evil. We can fear the devil and yet not fear his efforts to attack us, if we avail ourselves of God's trustworthy protection. A child who is terrified of a rattlesnake in the yard is not frightened when he is picked up and held safe, snuggling in his father's protective arms, distanced from the threat.

A trusting, warm fellowship with the Lord is the best protection from fearful demons. You may be severely tempted and harassed by forces of evil, as so many of the saints were; Jesus, himself, while in the desert, was tempted three times by Satan, and was confronted by him while performing exorcisms. As long as you stay close to God, however, trusting in his care, you cannot be enslaved by the Evil One. The devil himself knows that "you cannot partake of the table of the Lord and the table of demons" (1 Cor 10:21).

THREE

Detachment and Trust

On the morning of his execution, a death row inmate was offered a choice of menu for his last meal, according to the prison tradition. He requested scrambled eggs, but made only from Eggbeaters, not regular eggs. Asked why he refused ordinary eggs, he replied, "I'm watching my cholesterol."

There's a kind of absurdity in seeking long-range benefits when faced with a short-range opportunity to enjoy those benefits. Things that are important to us in life will be regarded as not all that necessary when viewed from our deathbed. At that momentous occasion, detachment from material things will not be much of a challenge. Menu decisions won't be as pressing as they once were, as the words of Jesus take on a deeper meaning: "Do not worry, saying, 'What will we eat?'...For it is the Gentiles who strive for all these things" (Mt 6:31-32). Vanity will not be an issue, with the immediate prospect of bodily decay. Amassing money won't be a driving desire, either, for, as the proverb says, "There are no pockets in a shroud." You can't take it with you. Detachment is a struggle in this life, but easy when we are about to leave it to be launched into eternity.

It wouldn't do us any harm if we could adopt now, while still fully alive, something of that deathbed detachment—minus any overtone of morbidity, of course. Job, in his desolation and forced detachment, still passed the test of *trusting in God* in his most ravaging deprivations. He didn't need to be taught how to relate the spirit of detachment to trust: "The LORD gave, and the LORD has taken away; blessed be the name of the LORD" (Jb 1:21).

The pagan Socrates chose to convert his spirit of attachment to that of detachment by dumping all of his money into the sea, in order to be totally undistracted from his pursuit of philosophy. How much more should we Christians, whose goal is to "strive first for the kingdom of God and his righteousness" (Mt 6:33), be ready to relinquish those material gifts, even while using them for his glory? When we *are* deprived, can we imitate Job by still praising the Lord?

FOUR

Faith and Trust

Think for a moment about the difference between these two sentences: "I believe in you" and "I believe you." The first remark attests to my faith in you as a reliable person, whereas the second refers to my faith in the reliability of your statements or assertions. Obviously there is a connection between the two remarks, since I can fully believe you only if I fully believe in you.

This analogy represents the primary and secondary forms of the virtue of faith, as described in the Vatican II *Decree on Divine Revelation.* By *primary* faith we believe in God, in the person of Jesus, as the Revealer of truth (see Jn 14:6), who reveals the Father's mind through the Spirit of truth (vv. 16-17). Yet by *secondary* faith we believe whatever he reveals to be true, especially as he reveals it through "the church of the living God, the pillar and the bulwark of the truth" (1 Tm 3:15).

Scripture often points out the clear relationship between *whom* we believe and *what* we believe; for example, John tells us that Jesus, "whom God has sent speaks the words of God" (Jn 3:34). When our belief (faith) is directed to the *person* of the deity rather than the revealed truths (teachings or doctrines) of that deity, then we refer to that dimension of faith as the virtue of *trust.*

The words "healthy" and "healthful" are often (wrongly) used interchangeably by persons who are not aware of the subtle nuances of the English language. Likewise, persons not aware of the nuances of words in theology often use the words *faith* and *trust* as if they were synonymous.

Trust is a special form of faith that is person-focused; it is distinguished from doctrinal faith, which is referred to generically as belief. Trust is a type of faith characterized by confident reliance on a sovereign being. Thus, to say meaningfully, "I trust in the Lord," is to experience a comfortable reliance on him that brings with it the privileged blessing referred to by Jeremiah (17:7): "Blessed are those who trust in the LORD, whose trust is the LORD."

Trusting in humans (e.g., "having faith" in the police or in a surgeon or a psychiatrist), is usually a good natural trait, but it's not the supernatural virtue we are dealing with here. The supernatural virtue requires that the trusted person must be sovereign and divine, as Paul reminds us: "Such is the confidence that we have *through Christ toward God*" (2 Cor 3:4, emphasis mine).

If you start with expectant faith in a prayer of petition, then you already have a kind of *belief* in a future favorable outcome. That particular non-doctrinal form of faith overlaps the virtue of hope (see the following chapter on hope and trust). Merely expecting an answer to a prayer of petition would be the charismatic *gift* of faith referred to in 1 Corinthians 12:9. In Hebrews 11:1 it is called "the assurance of things hoped for."

Yet even such hope-filled faith is not trust. To have authentic trust as a *virtue*, a person must not just believe in a favorable outcome (healing and so forth), but rather be primarily focused on the reliability of the One being petitioned; the expectancy must be personalized—that is, person-focused. Jesus highlights this issue succinctly and emphatically: "Do not let your hearts be troubled. Believe in *God*, believe also in *me*" (Jn 14:1, emphasis mine).

Failure to prioritize this personalization—a subtle requirement for trust—is why many faith-filled persons complain that their prayers are never answered. *Their mistake is in primarily believing that their request will be fulfilled, rather than primarily believing in the reliability of the One who will ful-*

fill it. (See my booklet and four-tape recording titled *When God Says No: Twenty-Five Reasons Why Some Prayers Are Not Answered,* distributed by CTM, Box 19100, Los Angeles, CA 90019-0100.)

In Hebrews 11:6, the author speaks about expectant faith—that is, faith that expects that one's prayers will be answered. He trenchantly asserts that without that expectant kind of faith, "it is impossible to please God." If you wonder why this expectant faith is indispensable for pleasing God (attaining holiness), then read carefully the rest of the sentence: "for whoever would approach him must believe that he exists and that he rewards those who seek him"—*not* those who simply seek a favor and have only a background awareness that he is the source of that favor. The words in this statement that are overlooked by most readers of the Bible are precisely those describing personalism, the very element of expectant faith that characterizes the true champions of the exquisite virtue of trust: "those who seek *him.*"

When this specific form of faith called trust flourishes in your soul, you should humbly recognize it as one of many special graces from God (see Jn 1:16), not something construed only by your goodwill or by your pious human efforts. In addition, for trust to thrive and grow, you must depend confidently on the divine Gardener to water and fertilize it, for God gives the growth (see 1 Cor 3:6).

FIVE

Hope and Trust

"Blessed are they who expect nothing, for they shall receive it." This faux beatitude must have been formulated by either a pessimist, a skeptic, or, more probably, a pessimistic skeptic.

Expectancy, like so many human states, can be either negative or positive. To habitually expect bad or neutral results to our endeavors is simply psychopathological negativism. In contrast, habitual expectance of favorable outcomes is a sign of an optimistic, upbeat, well-integrated personality. "You will live in hope if hope lives in you," says the old aphorism. Hope is also one of the premiere characteristics of the Christian philosophy of life. The biblical history of salvation chronicles many tumultuous human events, but closes by trumpeting the ultimate triumph of the answer to our ageless prayer: "Thy kingdom come."

If trust is one manifestation of faith, where does the virtue of hope fit into the picture? Faith and hope are linked, as it were, by trust. From the viewpoint of time, we might say that the virtue of faith is based on the present, while the virtue of hope is futuristic. The linkage consists in the fact that trust is a confident *present* belief that a reliable God will certainly provide a *future* favorable outcome. However, there's more to it than that.

The virtue of trust, while drawing its force from faith and hope, must be a positive and profound reliance on a loving, caring divine *Person* as the One who will provide that favorable outcome. We must be securely aware that the outcome or reward will not happen just because we have faith in our faith, or because we have doctrinal faith in the omnipotence of God. Believing that something *can* happen by God's power is not the same as believing that it *will* happen. Moreover, even having the virtue of hope—the belief that the hoped-for outcome *will* happen—will still not make that belief qualify as holy *trust*, even though it may involve strong expectancy.

Hence, the faith that believes, for instance, that a healing of cancer *can* happen, coupled with hope that expects that it *will* happen, still falls short of the virtue of trust. In this situation, the primary focus is simply devout *faith* in the possibility of the healing, coupled with a prayerful, confident *hope* in the eventuality of the healing. That's analogous to the faith and hope of a dog waiting for the bone held just out of its reach.

Yet only secondarily is the focus on the Person who brings

about the healing. The awareness of God's power and action is certainly present, but only as a kind of background awareness of God as the agent. What is the quintessential element that is missing that would make the prayer one of authentic trust? It is foreground awareness, not background awareness, of the fact that the prayed-for cure will come as an ineluctable flow of beneficence from the loving, nurturing divine *Person* who delights in providing such benefits for his beloved children. In the words of Jesus (Lk 11:13), "If you [earthly fathers]…know how to give good gifts to your children, how much more will the heavenly Father give…to those who ask him!" In this verse Jesus emphasizes reliance on a *personal* God as the "sublimator" of hope-filled faith. Only when that person-focus is operative can we speak of a *trustful* hope.

SIX

Love and Trust

Consider four situations in which you might exercise trust. First, it's very risky to entrust your life savings to a person who hates you. Second, it's less risky but still quite chancy to entrust your life savings to a stranger who neither loves nor hates you. Third, there is no risk in entrusting your money to a noble, virtuous person who loves you with the deepest heartfelt love and has frequently gifted you generously. And fourth, if the love between you and that treasured person is mutual, then the trust is optimal, and that person, with his or her quality of trustworthiness, is precious to you. Why? Because trust is coterminous with love. (See the first chapter of this book.)

Now, tighten your seat belt and ponder with me, if you will, step by step, this deep scriptural truth about love-fostered trust; you'll soon understand why it's a major shortcut to holiness. Let us start with the awesome fact that our good, kind, and merciful God loves each of us with an infinite and endless love. "I have loved you with an everlasting love; therefore I have continued my faithfulness to you" (Jer 31:3) ..."with cords of human kindness, with bands of love" (Hos 11:4). Simply look devoutly at a crucifix, as Paul suggests (see Gal 3:1), and ask yourself what besides love could motivate someone to choose such a torturous death for another. "No one has greater love than this" (Jn 15:13).

Thus we see no problem or limit on God's part of the equation. But what about our part? It's up to us to make the love between Creator and creature fully mutual, as stipulated by the famous law of reciprocity, first formulated by the "apostle of love": "We love because he first loved us" (1 Jn 4:19). Yet, to attain the kind of trust described in the fourth situation above, we must love back *as fully as possible*, so as not to leave his yearning for love unrequited: "Love the LORD your God *with all your heart, and with all your soul, and with all your might*" (Dt 6:5, emphasis mine). "The LORD takes pleasure in those ...who hope in his steadfast love" (Ps 147:11). Jesus reminds us that only this *mutual* love will lead to the mystical insights by which he will reveal himself to us (see Jn 14:20-21).

However, the question still remains: how does this *mutual love* relate to the *virtue of trust*? David articulated the answer as a prayer in Psalm 86:2-5 (emphasis added): "I am devoted to you; save your servant who *trusts* in you. You are my God; be gracious to me, O LORD, ... You, O LORD, are good and forgiving, *abounding in steadfast love* to all who call on you." In our love-response, our trust in God is equal to our love for him, since it is the primary expression of our love for him.

Yet it is John who answers this question about trust most incisively, including within his answer a reminder that authentic trust presupposes a lived love that soars beyond mere words: "Whoever lives in love lives in God, and God in him. In this way, [mutual] love is made complete among us so that we will have confidence" (1 Jn 4:16-17, NIV). It is this giving-receiving love that engenders in the soul a full-blossomed trust in God. That trust is so deep that the soul embraces God's will just as easily in his "no" as in his "yes" in answer to prayers of petition. In that stage of trust, the soul bounds like a gazelle among the peaks of holiness.

SEVEN

Suffering and Trust

One of my favorite squibs is the probing insight on the popular "bumper snicker": *If you feel far from God, guess who moved!*

If you feel far from God in the midst of your suffering, you're in good company; even the holy prophet Jeremiah moved away from God by doubting his trustworthiness: "Why is my pain unceasing...? Truly, you are to me like a deceitful brook, like waters that fail." (Jer 15:18). You may be thirsting for God's help, but, like Jeremiah, you may find God to be "like waters that fail" in the midst of the miseries and trials you're undergoing—and also the ones you fear in the uncertain future. You may truly want to maintain trust in divine providence amidst such agonizing situations as a multitude of physical ailments and pains, or emotional pressures like worry about the danger of being victimized by criminals or terrorists, fear of the meltdown of the economy, the struggle with overwhelming addictions, or the dread of death. There's even a deep suffering in concern about your loved ones losing their faith, their jobs, or their health. Holding on to your trust and confidence in the Lord's providence in situations like these is akin to trying to hold on to a squirming greased pig.

Hopefully, if you admit this weakness, your prayer will become that of the psalmist: "With my whole heart I seek you; do not let me stray from your commandments" (Ps 119:10). Probably, however, your prayer is distracted with the question, *How can I prevent the slippage of my trust in God, especially in the midst of my trials and tribulations?* How does one acquire unfaltering trust in God in every event of life, and become acutely aware of—and submit to—his divine trustworthiness? The answer, of course, is that simple word: *trust*. Plead for that gift often, even daily; we never have enough of it.

EIGHT

Adversity and Trust

One of the most difficult challenges we face in our spiritual life is trusting in God's loving providence when we are hurt by the malice of other humans. It's one of the most anguishing tests of our spiritual maturity. Trusting God to bring good from evil is in itself not too difficult—unless we are the targets of that evil. Then it becomes considerably more difficult. Almost anyone can fulfill the Bible's command, "Do not fret because of evil-doers" (Prv 24:19). Yet that injunction can come to mean little or nothing to someone who has had a loved one murdered, or who has been tortured, robbed, or cheated out of a job. Punishment for evil we must leave to God (who sometimes exercises it partly through civil sanctions like imprisonment).

Learning to trust God when we are victimized requires taking some steps that will predispose us to that trust. Our first step should be to refuse to play God. "Never avenge yourselves, but leave room for the wrath of God; for it is written, 'Vengeance is mine, I will repay,' says the Lord.... Do not be overcome by evil, but overcome evil with good" (Rom 12:19, 21).

Our second step in disposing ourselves to trust in God in situations of human hurt is to obey Jesus' fourfold command regarding those who hurt us (see Lk 6:27-28): first, love your enemies (with benevolent or agape love, not necessarily liking them, but desiring good for them, such as their repentance and salvation); second, do good to them (at least by civil courtesy, if not warm kindness); third, call down God's blessings on them—in Peter's words, "Repay with a blessing" (1 Pt 3:9); and finally, pray for them.

If we ignore these four demands Jesus gave us regarding our enemies, we'll never learn to trust God, because our sin of unforgiveness will distance us from him who said, "if you do not forgive others, neither will your Father forgive your trespasses" (Mt 6:15). If you can't trust his revelation about dealing with your victimizers, you can't trust him to make your victimization eventuate in good.

As an example, think of how Joseph's trust in God when persecuted redounded to saving a nation from starvation. Joseph told his brothers, "Even though you intended to do harm to me, God intended it for good, in order to preserve a numerous people" (Gn 50:20). To trust God in hurtful situations, we must keep in mind that God does not approve the sin by which we are hurt, but he does *permissively* will the harm that results from the sin—a harm that in his eyes is a means to draw us closer to him or to bring some other good. "Does disaster befall a city, unless the LORD has done it?" (Am 3:6).

God may permit and sometimes even cause pain through others (without causing the malice itself). Trust enables us to see that pain as if it were caused by a surgeon, using surgical instruments. Mary, at the foot of the cross, saw evil men acting as the instruments of God's great act of redemption. One of the marvels of the Lord's ingenuity is his ability to make the evil of humans redound to the good of the victims who submit to his circuitous ways.

NINE

Trials and Trust

The word "trial" can mean "ordeal," or it can mean something quite different, namely, "test." Our hardships can be approached from either point of view, but we tend to emphasize the "ordeal" rather than the more positive "test." Yet, in the divine plan, every trial in our lives is a critical test of our trust in the providence that allows or causes it for our good.

Full-blown trust is so reliant on God's faithfulness that those who experience it regard it as almost insulting to ask

God "why?" when faced with hard-to-understand situations. Because they are convinced that "the Lord knows how to rescue the godly from trial" (2 Pt 2:9), those who completely trust in the Lord are like airplane passengers calmly riding out the momentary turbulence because they are sure that the pilot knows how to handle the situation.

After landing, our experience of a turbulent flight dissolves into the heap of vague memories of past disturbances. In retrospect, our trials don't appear to have been all that disturbing. Interestingly, we seem to have more trust in the pilot after the flight than we did during the trip. Viewed from eternity, our present trials will all look like false alarms. Just realizing that truth, and recalling it often, can make our trust in the Lord considerably easier to develop.

TEN

Tribulations and Trust

"In the day of my trouble I call on you, for you will answer me" (Ps 86:7). When God answers our call for his help in the midst of anguishing tribulations, we might find that his answer is really more, not less, than we ask for. The answer sometimes comes not in the form of relief, but in that of belief—namely, belief that he wants us to grow stronger, not weaker, in the tribulations and adversities of life. For truly trusting souls, the answer may come by way of a powerful gift of insight—a profound enlightenment that enables us to see how gently he guides each tribulation into a transformation. He helps us by such painful steps to be "transformed by the renewing of your minds" (Rom 12:2). The trusting soul quickly perceives the Lord's subtle ways of transmuting tribulations into learning experiences.

The Israelites would probably have been ill-prepared to appreciate and use the benefits of the Promised Land of

Canaan if they had not undergone the great tribulations of their wilderness journey. Moses, in the epilogue of his great song (see Dt 32), told the people to expect this outcome to their sufferings in the desert. Without the cross there is no crown.

Matthew Henry, in his *Commentary on Scripture*, proclaimed this truth with his typical eloquence:

> Many are taught with the briars and thorns of affliction that otherwise would not learn. God gives wisdom by the rod and reproof; he chastens and teaches as he opens our ears to discipline.... Let every pricking briar and grieving thorn, especially when it is a thorn in the flesh, be thus interpreted and thus improve us. By this God deigns to teach us. Shall we learn by his mysterious teaching?

To accept the mystery of suffering requires a trust that is unshakeable, like that of Job, who declared, "Though he slay me, yet I will trust him" (Jb 13:15 NKJV). The resultant mystical insight that he experienced was followed by an overwhelming reward (see Jb 42). This was not so much a reward for his suffering as it was for his trust in God in the midst of suffering.

ELEVEN
Problems and Trust

Even oldsters may have forgotten that there was once a popular TV program called *Father Knows Best*. The phrase is schmaltzy, perhaps, but there's a profound truth in these simple words when they refer to our heavenly Father, who always knows best. Our challenge is to let ourselves be really convinced of that verity. A loving, concerned parent will cause a tiny child to cry by taking away the sharp knife or matches with which he's playing, though the child can't see the reason for being thus deprived. It was the parent's love that brought about the child's frustration, but that love is not obvious to the child. If we could see our problem situations as God sees them, we would answer our own prayers as God sometimes does, with a loving "no."

Since we can't see things as God does, even though we may acknowledge that his wisdom is far superior to ours, we still must decide whether or not we will submit to his wise plan. If we do submit, we may do so reluctantly if our faith is anemic; or, if we are more mature, we may submit joyfully. Yet even joyful submission is not full-fledged trust. As tribulation continues, we may try to justify ourselves: "I cry to you and you do not answer me; / ... / You have turned cruel to me" (Jb 30:20-21). If, like Job, we fail to see and appreciate God's *love* behind the permitted hardship, we may succeed in submission but fail in authentic trust. That very awareness of God's love in permitting our suffering isn't a self-activated insight; it results only from humble prayer asking God to show us his love in our pain.

Eliphaz showed Job, as the Lord also did later, that the very questioning of God's plan shows both pride and a lack of faith. Job finally humbled himself in his anguish, and with God's special revelation he reached beyond submission to complete trust. It might have been easier for him if he had had access to Jeremiah's revelation: "Although he causes grief, he will have compassion according to the abundance of his *steadfast* love; for he does not willingly afflict or grieve anyone" (Lam 3:32-33, emphasis mine). If we keep this in mind it is easier to use trust as the handle by which we take hold of God's promises and apply them to our daily problems.

Ultimately our biggest difficulty is dealing with problems problematically. That is, we seek solutions to our problems more earnestly than we seek the divine problem-solver himself. This is a basic failure in trust that bespeaks an anemic spiritual life; its result is that often our petitions are rendered ineffective. Yet, ever patient as he is, the Lord waits for us to "seek his presence" (Ps 105:4) sincerely and earnestly, so that he can open to us the cornucopia of his beneficence. He will display it here on earth as a tempting glimpse and foretaste of the lavish menu planned for us in his heavenly banquet.

TWELVE
Pressure and Trust

A few years ago in Virginia an explosion occurred in a most unusual location for such an incident: in a garbage truck! Nearby office buildings were evacuated and two firefighters hospitalized due to the release of a poisonous gas. An investigation showed that the explosion was the result of the compacting of a substance disposed of as garbage, namely calcium hypochlorite, a powdered form of chlorine, which normally is harmlessly dissolved in swimming pools.

This occurrence could well be a point of comparison for the effect of life's normal activities. If they are dissolved and diffused through normal performance of duties, they are characterized by energy, vigor, and vitality for accomplishing things. Yet if put under excessive pressure, ordinary activities can explode into dangerous problems—physical, emotional, and even spiritual. Generally, we refer to this as stress.

In a Harvard study sponsored by the American Psychiatric Association, it was shown that recently divorced persons are five times more likely to be involved in fatal car accidents than are others who are not under the stress of adjusting to the trauma of divorce. Similar high-pressure situations, such as job stress, being fired, breakup of a love affair, quarrels, overwork, and so on, are responsible for more traffic fatalities than is abuse of alcohol (although substance abuse is itself, consciously or subconsciously, used as a means to diminish or escape stress). Thousands upon thousands of clinical tests have definitively shown that the pressures of life, if not coped with adequately, will inevitably be deleterious to one's physical or mental health in any of hundreds of ways.

More and more we find the medical profession exploring forms of spiritual exercises as antidotes to the poisonous effects of stress. Some of these spiritual approaches may themselves be dangerous, especially when they are derived from New Age tenets. Yet other spiritual approaches are not only safe but truly therapeutic, such as authentic prayer that is not an abstract uplifting of the mind to some force or architectonic energy but a prayer directed to a personal, loving God who is not to be feared but *loved and trusted in total abandonment.*

No religious movement or organization fulfills these ideal conditions better than Christianity. This is especially true when the Christian prayer is not limited to a mere petition for help, but is primarily a contemplative act of quiet worship, adoration, gratitude, and especially a trusting reliance on God as non-threatening and merciful, supportive, compassionate, healing, and loving. There is no better exercise to counteract stress than learning to relax in God's arms like a baby in the loving embrace of a nurturing mother or father. This is simply enjoying a prolonged divine hug. That is the simplest act of creature-Creator trust possible. It is not only the most therapeutic means of stress reduction, it is also the most grace-laden.

THIRTEEN

Persecution and Trust

On the rear of a battered car I saw a "bumper snicker" that managed to combine humor and arrogance: "If you don't like the way I drive, stay off the sidewalk." In spite of its nuance of humor, it trenchantly articulated the "get-out-of-my-way" mentality that underlies much of the crime rampant in our society. And for every crime there's a victim.

It's those countless victims of multifarious evil who most often ask the question, "Why does God allow evil persons to do such harm to others?" That very question shows how distant is the human awareness that God is still in charge, and that he actually can and does bring good out of evil (see Rom 8:28). With that basic truth out of our mental range, trusting God in the face of malicious persecution seems more foolish than virtuous.

God's permissive will (not his positive will) allows evil persons to do harm to us, even allows Satan and demons to attack us (see Jb 1:12 and 2:6). Jesus himself was the victim of evil persons who engineered his death, and was also assailed by Satan himself in the desert. Through the centuries God has, by his permissive will, allowed boundless wickedness to flourish by the malice of humans.

Thus, rape, war, theft, terrorism, and the like are clearly not God's positive will, but they are operative under his permissive will (see Prv 16:4). He hates such malevolent behavior, but he permits it so as not to vitiate the very essence of human nature by interfering with any person's freedom to choose to do evil (for that would also freeze that person's freedom to choose to do good). Yet he defends and vindicates the righteous victims: "Commit your way to the LORD; trust in him, and he will act. He will make your vindication shine like the light, and the justice of your cause like the noonday" (Ps 37:5-6).

The soul with profound trust in God in the face of widespread malevolence sees such permitted-but-not-desired evil as part of the universal workplace of Providence—part of the "all things" that Paul refers to in his classic formulation of divine providence: "We know that all things work together for good for those who love God, who are called according to his purpose" (Rom 8:28). His "purpose" is his providential design by which he enables good to come from evil, without approving or rewarding the evil itself. Souls who enjoy an ample degree of trust accept this truth, even when, like Job (see 42:3), they can't grasp the divine ingenuity behind such a purpose (see Prv 16:4).

Our acceptance of God's permissive will, which *permits* us to be victimized by burglary, rape, acts of terrorism, and the like, does not contravene our obligation to strive to prevent, suppress, or punish such crimes or acts of wickedness. Hence the need for police, courts, fines, prison sentences, and so on. Our effort to suppress evil is part of God's *positive* will for us. "I shall have an answer for those who taunt me, for I trust in your word" (Ps 119:42). "Rescue me, O my God, from the hand of the wicked, from the grasp of the unjust and cruel" (Ps 71:4).

The whole dynamic of the agelessly questioned problem of evil provides a most difficult challenge in practicing the virtue of trust in God. Unless we are given Job's miraculous mystical insight into God's plan and purpose of innocent people suffering (Jb 42:5), we must fall back on unquestioning *trust* in God's wisdom and love until the Day of the Lord, when he'll restore all things to himself. Then we won't need faith; we'll have direct knowledge (see Ez 6:10). As Paul puts it, "Now I know only in part; then I will know fully" (1 Cor 13:12).

Real trust in God enables us to endure false accusations with the confident expectation that ultimately God will clear our names, as he did with David and other luminaries of the Bible who suffered persecution: "they persecuted the prophets who were before you" (Mt 5:12). A true Christian even expects persecution: "If they persecuted me, they will persecute you" (Jn 15:20).

Yet part of our trust in the face of such assault is the conviction that God will not let this form of suffering go unrewarded: "Blessed are you when people revile you and persecute you and utter all kinds of evil against you falsely on my account. *Rejoice and be glad*, for your reward is great in heaven" (Mt 5:11-12, emphasis mine). This promise provides a crucial and very challenging test of our sincerity in trusting in the Lord. To rejoice at being insulted and persecuted is humanly impossible except for those humble souls who trust in the Lord for the "great reward"; a person who is weak in trust can hardly even tolerate with equanimity an insult or persecution, much less "rejoice and be glad." As Jesus says, "when trouble or persecution arises…that person immediately falls away" (Mt 13:21).

FOURTEEN
Fear and Trust

The mythical story is as old as the messages on my answering machine, but it's worth retelling. It has to do with a frustrated hiker who approached a chasm he couldn't cross. He saw a daredevil acrobat crossing it on a tightrope above hundreds of feet of empty space while pushing a woman in a wheelbarrow. When the hiker complimented the acrobat on his balancing skill, the performer said he had safely performed the feat countless times with the woman, who was his wife. "I'll give you thousand-to-one odds that I can do it again," wagered the acrobat.

"I'm sure you can do it," said the hiker.

Then came the acrobat's challenging invitation: "If you're that sure, and really want to get to the other side, then get in the wheelbarrow!"

I think that must have been the same mythical hiker described in the similar and often-told story of how, having slipped off of a cliff, a man was hanging by an outcropping root while screaming, "Is there anyone up there to help me?" A divine voice from heaven asked if he would trustingly do *anything* required. The frantic man replied affirmatively, and was then told to let go. After a long pause, he called out, "Is there anyone else up there?"

We all like to boast that we trust God, who is more trustworthy than any mere human helper. Yet when we're really put to the test, our trust often proves weak; we're afraid to get in the wheelbarrow, and we're afraid to really let go, in spite of countless assurances of God's Word that we need not fear because of God's absolute trustworthiness. "Fear and trembling come upon me," admitted David (Ps 55:5), but he faced that fear and then, by God's grace, he rose above it: "When I am afraid I put my trust in you.... In God I trust; I *am not* afraid" (56:3, 11, emphasis mine). High-caliber trust is refusing to panic when things seem out of our control, because we know they are never out of God's control.

Thus, within that very same psalm, we see a subtle growth in David's outlook that is reminiscent of Spurgeon's classic two-level distinction in the faith-grounded virtue of trust. He observes that it is possible to get to heaven by traveling either first class or second class. "Second class travelers are those who trust when they fear; first class are those who trust and *don't* fear." David moved up from fear to nonfear: "When I am afraid I will trust" became "I will trust and not be afraid." In mid-flight, as it were, he chose to upgrade from coach to first-class.

"For you did not receive a spirit of slavery to fall back into fear, but you have received a spirit of adoption. When we cry, 'Abba! Father!' it is that very Spirit bearing witness with our spirit that we are children of God, and if children, then heirs, heirs of God and joint heirs with Christ" (Rom 8:15-17). Once we have accepted Christ and as long as we remain aligned with God's will, we need not fear punishment from God, nor should we fear God himself—other than by "fear of the LORD," which is a fear or dread of offending him, that is, a reverent respect for him (see chapter 69 of this book).

Love should eclipse all morbid fear, as St. John reminds us: "There is no fear in love, but perfect love casts out fear; for fear has to do with punishment, and whoever fears has not reached perfection in love" (1 Jn 4:18). Anyone who really loves God trusts him totally, and it is that very trusting love that "casts out fear."

From this observation, it can be deduced that the more we fear, the less we trust. The phrases "fear not," "do not be afraid," "why do you fear?" and the like appear 365 times in the Bible, and most often they refer to freedom from fear and anxiety as related to one's trust in God. Jesus himself often affirmed this idea: "Do not let your hearts be troubled. Trust in God" (Jn 14:1, NIV).

FIFTEEN
Worry and Trust

Imagine Jesus appearing to you and giving you a specific command to avoid something, and then restating that command five more times. You would certainly take that admonition seriously. This is exactly what Jesus did when he delivered a forceful sermon condemning worry as a sign of lack of trust in him. You can read about this in Matthew 6:25-34, where six times Jesus forbids us to worry. There's no better self-examination on the virtue of trust than a review of what we worry about, and for what stretches of time we engage in worry.

Here is something to really worry about: If you are worried for five minutes, then for those five minutes you are not fully in God's will. For those five minutes you do not truly trust him. Likewise, if you worry for three days, then for those three days you are not fully in God's will, for you have let the LORD's presence and his reliability slip far into the background of your consciousness. Jesus said godless people think this way (see Mt 6:32). Why? Because it manifests a weakness or sometimes an absence of that God-focused form of faith that is called trust. A guru said it philosophically: "Don't be afraid of the day you have never seen." An aphorism I once saw on a calendar page said it more theologically: "Never be afraid to trust the unknown future to a known God."

Nevertheless, we must not confuse worry with legitimate concern. Concern for the millions of starving people in the world is not a self-centered thought, but a mental act of charity and altruism. Concern for the health of your loved ones or concern for employment to provide a livelihood for your family is also altruistic, for the most part. This is even truer if one's concern is for the repentance, sanctification, or salvation of others—especially a relative or close friend. That would be the virtue of zeal, which, as a form of charity, is a desire for someone's spiritual good.

However—and this is a point often disregarded—if that concern exists as *an unsettling inner experience* ("troubled" is the word Jesus uses in John 14:27), then it seriously corrodes one's spiritual life. This troubled mentality has little or no reference to a reliance on the Lord to ultimately take care of the situation with his prayer-drawn grace. For that reason, it is no longer a virtuous concern, but a fault of worry, roundly condemned by Jesus in his gospel message.

How does one distinguish clearly between sinful worry and virtuous concern? There are two primary characteristics of virtuous concern. First, the mind keeps the matter God-focused with quiet, calm petition, while maintaining awareness that the heavenly Father himself knows our needs (see Mt 6:32) and is concerned with them (see 1 Pt 5:7 and Ps 55:22). Second, a concern that is truly not worrisome is characterized by a deep serenity—that is, an emotional tranquility (peace of heart) and a spiritual tranquility (peace of soul). This peace of soul (see chapter 70 of this book) is a fruit of the Spirit (see Gal 5:22) and is a special supernatural gift that comes to us only from Jesus: "*My* peace I give to you. I do not give to you as the world gives. *Do not let your hearts be troubled* [i.e., worried], and do not let them be afraid" (Jn 14:27, emphasis mine). In more colloquial terms: Don't lose any sleep worrying. Give it to God. He's up all night anyway!

SIXTEEN
Anxiety and Trust

A four-year-old reported to his mother that his toothbrush had fallen into the toilet. She fished it out and gingerly deposited it into the garbage can. A few minutes later, he brought her another toothbrush—her own—and said, "You'd better throw this one away too. It fell in the toilet last week."

No one needs to be convinced that life is a series of problems. To paraphrase an old saying, "If it's not one darn thing, it's two!" There's always a problem to be solved, and there are always problems to worry about that will soon need to be solved, even if we don't yet know what they are. It's those future, as yet nonexistent, problems that cause us to worry or experience anxiety—the antithesis of peace. We need to experience an ongoing peace that dispels the darkness of anxiety. Yet negative upstages positive in our society (that's why the thesaurus has 17 words for an honest person and 193 for a dishonest one), and what is worse, the negative, such as anxiety, often has a disproportionately minor cause.

The National Institute of Mental Health reports that about one person in every eight has the most common form of mental illness, chronic anxiety disorder, in one of its various forms: panic disorder, phobias, undifferentiated anxiety, social anxiety (shyness), post-traumatic stress disorder, obsessive compulsive disorder, or major depression. Women more than men and children more than adults are subject to these various forms of anxiety.

Neurologists today have a deeper knowledge of the causes of anxiety than they did a few years ago. Here is an absurdly oversimplified view of this new knowledge: A real or imagined threat excites fear in the brain's amygdala. That activates the hippocampus, which registers the emotion-laden memory of the threat, until and unless the prefrontal cortex kicks in with calming messages to quell the amygdala's fright. If the amygdala—the accelerator—is overactive, or if the cortex, or thinking part—the brake—is underactive, the result is chronic anxiety. Pharmaceuticals can slow the accelerator, while psychotherapy can improve the brake in the cortex. Therapy can alleviate the problem; but besides this, not instead of it, there is a deeper solution: learning peace-inducing trust in God.

In these cataclysmic times our most enviable fellow humans are those who can somehow find joy in the joyless hurts of life, and peace in the midst of turbulence. Most of us are atrophied, faith-weak souls, who cannot find solace in the ultimate promise that "all the ends of the earth shall see the salvation of our God" (Is 52:10). The real faith champions are those who find eye-of-the-hurricane tranquility in the simple assurance of God's comforting word: "The Lord is near. Do not worry about anything" (Phil 4:5-6). *"Cast all your anxiety on him*, because he cares for you" (1 Pt 5:7, emphasis mine; see Ps 55:22).

Total freedom from anxiety is found in perfect trust in God: "Those of steadfast mind you keep in peace—in peace because they *trust* in you" (Is 26:3, emphasis mine). Perfect trust is a love-assured and recklessly trusting self-abandonment to divine providence—a providence that itself is recognized as both loving and trustworthy. Job in his anguish came close to this when he exclaimed: "Though he slay me, yet will I trust him" (Jb 13:15 NKJV). Actually, Job didn't practice *full* trust, although he did show submission; that is, he acknowledged the wisdom and power in God's providence, but he had difficulty perceiving love in that divine providence—like so many today who admit God's wisdom and power but challenge his love in the face of problems like wars, starvation, unanswered prayer, and the like.

If one's anxiety is of a neurological origin, or the result of insecurity from having been emotionally traumatized, as in the psychopathological condition known as post-traumatic stress disorder, then of course professional therapy is called for, including properly prescribed psychopharmaceuticals. (For the scriptural basis for medical treatment, see Sir 38:1-16.) This is not to discount the numerous examples of miraculously healed persons with anxiety neurosis—patients who prayerfully sought God's great gift of inner peace (see Jn 14:27) by fostering consummate trust in the tender, loving Lord of creation. The attitude of unflagging trust in our heavenly Father can result in its own intrinsic therapy. Such calm trust, *if sustained*, is "God's tranquilizer." When unrelenting (see Ps 86:3), it can quell the torment of anxiety-ridden souls.

SEVENTEEN
Belief and Trust

While engaged in my hobby of bookstore browsing, a book of phrases caught my attention because it gave a humorous twist to biblical phrases. One phrase that evoked a chuckle was, "O ye of little faith," with its definition: "Those who look both ways before crossing a one-way street."

I'm sure that taking extra precautions in a dangerous world is not a bad idea. Yet some situations do not allow us to see all sides of a situation, even when some hidden views are God's design for us. If you were allowed to see only the back-side of an exquisite tapestry, it wouldn't look very beautiful; you would see a hodgepodge of colored thread without anything to inspire artistic appreciation. It's only when the tapestry is viewed from the front side, as intended, that the beauty of its delicate detail can be appreciated.

The Divine Weaver is in the process of making a gorgeous tapestry of the thread of your life. Every one of your acts of kindness, courtesy, humility, patience, or prayer is a thread woven into this splendid *objet d'art*. It can be seen and marveled at from heaven's point of view—the front side. You will see it that way only later, however, when you cross the threshold of eternity. For now, your appreciation of the piece of work is simply a trusting belief that the Weaver is at work on something surprisingly magnificent.

This distortion of our present view of spiritual realities is perhaps simply part of God's plan to make heaven's "surprise party" more exciting. It is his way of testing our belief as we trust the Lord to keep a "scorecard"—"the Lamb's book of life"

(Rv 21:27)—recording everything we have done in life to further God's glory by our acts of virtue. Hebrews 6:10 reminds us that "God is not unjust; he will not overlook your work and the love that you showed for his sake in serving the saints, as you still do." Your belief system must include a confident trust that he's planning something beautiful to show you about yourself. Trust him to do this, as his holy Word promises, and get ready to enjoy eternally a magnificent work of art!

EIGHTEEN
Temptation and Trust

It has been said that humans are subject to three kinds of temptation: to shine, to whine and to recline. The first one—to shine—comprises all temptations to pride in its many forms, including vanity, resentment, unforgiveness of one's enemies, arrogance, argumentativeness, refusal to apologize, and so on. The second—to whine—includes all temptations to negativism, such as complaint, discouragement, despair, weakening of faith because of God's lack of answer to prayer, and so on. The third—to recline—epitomizes all temptations to sloth, lack of zeal for evangelizing others or for God's glory, disinterestedness in virtue, and neglect of one's countless responsibilities or duties (moral, professional, and so on).

Temptation is multifarious, mathematically equal to the number of possible failures or weaknesses that assail us faltering mortals. Temptation is present whenever a moral choice, or even a spiritual choice, is to be made. Hence, the choice may not always be a serious matter, involving a raw selection between good and evil. Quite often it will be a more subtle type of choice—that between a lower and a higher good, such as that between mediocrity and the "Be perfect" challenge of Jesus in Matthew 5:48. Such a subtle option could be a preference for "little with righteousness" (Prv 16:8) as against "complete and perfect fidelity" (Ti 2:10).

The most common category of temptation is the choice between satisfaction with mediocrity, on the one hand, and, on the other, the pursuit of perfection in any aspect of life. The "if you wish to be perfect" option that Jesus offers (Mt 19:21) is often counterpointed by his reproach of the church in Sardis ("I have not found your works perfect in the sight of my God" [Rv 3:2]) and of the church in Laodicea ("You are neither cold nor hot. I wish that you were either cold or hot" [v. 15]).

The effort to choose the better part, like Mary in the house of Lazarus (see Lk 10:42), is the best (though not the only) *proof of love for God*; that's why the paycheck is sizeable: "Blessed is anyone who endures temptation. Such a one has stood the test and will receive the crown of life that the Lord has promised to *those who love him*" (Jas 1:12, emphasis mine).

The trust component in this matter of temptation is to be found in trusting the Lord for the strength to cope successfully with any temptation, but also in trusting that your efforts will not be without the hundredfold reward. When that double indicator of trust is present in temptation, you can know that you are truly trusting in the Lord.

NINETEEN

Self-Deception and Trust

There is a dimension of faith that consists of simply trusting in the Word of God that reminds us that when we feel worthless, God does not regard us with such negativity. In his eyes, we are actually priceless treasures, precious to him beyond estimation. This expression of trust is simply believing that the most talented, popular people in the world are no more lovable in God's eyes than we are in our plainness and ordinariness. The Lord watches over us no less than over the most saintly person. "Are not two sparrows sold for a penny? Yet not one of them will fall to the ground apart from your Father.... So do not be afraid; you are of more value than many sparrows" (Mt 10:29-31).

By this unique form of trust, we can come to recognize with unwavering certitude that we are valuable in God's eyes, even with our weaknesses and illnesses. He knows everything about us (see Mt 10:30), including our desires (see Ps 37:4). Moreover, he has a strategy in mind for each of us: "'For surely I know the plans I have for you,' says the LORD, 'plans for your welfare and not for harm, to give you a future with hope'" (Jer 29:11). He does not judge us because of what we can or cannot do (see Eph 2:8–9).

Jesus declared that all he did and said came from the One who sent him (see Jn 7:16). Hence, God works through Jesus and therefore he views us through the person of Jesus, whose presence permeates us, for he said, "Abide in me as I abide in you" (Jn 15:4). Thus, we can *trust* God to focus on the Christ presence within us, as he echoes his own words of affirmation: "You are my son, the Beloved; with you I am well pleased" (Mk 1:11). That kind of trust, gilded with humility, will preclude every form of self-deception.

TWENTY

Self-Discipline and Trust

A little girl said to her mother, "I'm happier today than I was yesterday." In response to the mother's inevitable "Why?" the moppet pondered for a moment before replying. Then she said, "Yesterday my thoughts pushed me around, but today I pushed my thoughts around."

That unsophisticated description of self-discipline is, I'm sure, as good as any. Controlling one's thoughts is the very *raison d'être* of self-discipline. Yet it is not as easy as you might imagine. Self is a kind of disease that we must strive to control throughout our lifetime. "I have had more trouble with myself than with anyone," admitted the renowned preacher Dwight Moody. A corollary to that is Tolstoy's observation: "Everybody thinks of changing humanity, and nobody thinks of changing himself." Everyone wants to have a share in the big omelet of the commonweal, but no one wants to break his own egg.

Self-discipline has three distinct connotations: the first is the notion of self-punishment—masochistic mortification designed to remove guilt even without sincere repentance. (Witness the self-flagellation or crucifixion cults in some third-world countries.) The second connotation sees self-discipline as a corrective process to strengthen and mold the individual to fit into some required social or cultural pattern, such as super-strict dress codes for office workers, or more heinously, strict coven attendance by Satanists or finger amputation or self-mutilation to indicate gang membership, and so on. The third connotation is the only one that makes self-discipline a virtue: it is a quality by which the individual cultivates certain ethical and moral standards of conduct that he or she is prepared to adhere to unflinchingly, in all circumstances, regardless of any foreseen or unforeseen painful consequences.

Without trusting the Lord and his revealed norms of morality to provide guidance in authentic self-discipline, one could fall into aberrations ranging all the way from pious but self-torturing scrupulosity to blasphemous satanic ritualism, and countless behavioral distortions in between. Moreover, the Lord must provide true motivation, not only to start but also to complete the work of self-reformation, which is ultimately *his* work from start to finish. With consummate trust in him, we will have no doubt whatsoever that "the one who began a good work among you will bring it to completion" (Phil 1:6).

TWENTY-ONE
Self-Sufficiency and Trust

Striving for absolute self-sufficiency is a vice, not a virtue. When you have no one in your life that you can call and say, "I'm scared," then your life is empty, isolated, unrelational, and unfulfilling. You need somebody you can trust enough to say, "I need help!"

If you truly recognize that you need help, it's easy to find. Simply accept the loving invitation of our comforting Savior: "Come to me, all you that are weary and are carrying heavy burdens, and I will give you rest" (Mt 11:28). If you are still hesitant, then pay heed to his more emphatic words about misdirected self-sufficiency: "I am the vine, you are the branches. Those who abide in me and I in them bear much fruit, because *apart from me you can do nothing*. Whoever does not abide in me is thrown away…and withers; such branches are gathered, thrown into the fire, and burned" (Jn 15:5-6, emphasis mine).

Dependence on the Lord involves pervasive trust on our part, of course. Yet, paradoxically, while we depend on him, he has also chosen to depend on *us*; that is, he depends on us for the accomplishment of his plans. He even pays us for our labor: "You have been trustworthy in a few things, I will put you in charge of many things; enter into the joy of your master" (Mt 25:21).

TWENTY-TWO
Self-Abandonment and Trust

Natives of some South Sea Islands use a unique method of capturing monkeys. They cut a small hole in the top of a coconut and insert some nuts inside, then chain the coconut to a tree trunk. The monkeys instinctively reach into the hollowed out coconut and grasp a fistful of nuts, but find that their closed fists full of nuts are too large to pull out of the small hole. Yet the monkeys refuse to release their fistfuls of nuts, so they are easily captured.

Like the stupid monkeys, many humans refuse to let go. They cling to their worries, their problems, and their fears, and never seem to be able to let go of these negative burdens and let God handle them. They would rather struggle than surrender.

This surrender or relinquishment of our problems to the Lord is ultimately not just abandonment of our negativity, but abandonment of our very self to the Lord in holy trust. Such total and unremitting self-abandonment is not a form of weakness but of strength. It's not a cowardly refusal to struggle with life's unfavorable issues; it's a strong reliance on the Lord rather than on ourselves. The motto of a spiritual movement called "Let's Be Saints" is the slogan, *"Let go—let God!"* It epitomizes, in the context of consummate trust, the noble virtue of self-abandonment to the Lord—a virtue that delights him immensely, and one that reaps a special heavenly reward.

When facing the adversities of life, our usual tendency is to hold on and struggle, worry, manipulate, and fight our way out of the adversity by ourselves. Often, it isn't until we become weary in our struggles and can see no other solution that we're forced to let go and let God work things out *his* way. The Lord is patiently watching us in our lonely, self-occupied struggle and beckons us to *just let go* so that he can handle the matter. Then, and only then, can we be free from the stress of worrisome issues. Even though we can't see what lies ahead, God knows his plans for our future and is holding us in the palm of his hand.

The Gaelic godsend formulates this as a prayer: "May the Lord keep you in the palm of his hand, and never close his fist!" We need not try to control the uncontrollable; he takes care of that impossibility. Trusting in him affords us the delight of living peacefully in the embrace of his ceaseless love and unrelenting support. If you want the best, let the Lord do the shopping!

TWENTY-THREE
Mediocrity and Trust

The ancient philosopher Epictetus provided some of the best motivational psychology of his day. He said, "First say to yourself what you would be. And then do what you have to do." That's simply gearing your thoughts to a proposed goal and then taking practical steps to make it a reality. Remember that establishing a goal in itself is not sufficient; you can't learn to drive a car or play the piano by simply desiring those goals; you have to actually drive or actually play the piano until the desired goal is achieved.

Spiritual mediocrity in an otherwise high-minded person is usually the result of sincerely aspiring to holiness without implementing the means to attain it. If left to itself, such complacency will eventually anesthetize the soul; it will tend to cause the person so afflicted to forget or even ignore altogether the Lord's pervasive and uninterrupted support and beneficence. The antidote to spiritual mediocrity and self-complacency is simply to "launch out into the deep" with surges of humble trust in the Lord. This will not only provide a God-designed protection against petty self-complacency but also further our growth by leaps and bounds.

Pope John XXIII, shortly before his death, said, "I believe that when I stand before God, he will simply ask me: How did you use the gifts of life that I gave you?" Jesus came that we "may have life, and have it abundantly" (Jn 10:10). If we don't accept and use that abundance, we will have to give an account of our neglected stewardship of his graces and blessings.

For a truly trusting soul, however, no grace or blessing falls through the cracks. A child who trusts his mother for sufficient food would never be deprived of nourishment by her: "Can a woman forget her nursing child, or show no compassion for the child of her womb? Even these may forget, yet I will not forget you" (Is 49:15). Nothing motivates God to

34

express his love for us more tenderly than when he sees us trusting him for all our needs. The reason for this is simply that by trusting him we are implicitly acknowledging our most basic creatural dependence on him as our Creator, Redeemer, Forgiver, Healer, Sustainer, Protector, and Guide.

TWENTY-FOUR
Prosperity and Trust

St. Alphonsus Liguori was known for his unconventional statements. He once remarked, "In building, we need not act as worldly people do. They first procure money, and then proceed to build. But we do the opposite. We begin to build and then as we go along we trust divine Providence to provide what is necessary." Of course, anyone who uses that approach without having a trust in God that is exceptional and rock solid will soon become bankrupt.

St. Frances Xavier Cabrini once remarked, "I have started community houses with no more than prayer and the price of a loaf of bread, for with him who comforts and supports me, I can do anything." Her astonishing outreach in helping the poor is regarded today as legendary, as was her trust in the Lord.

If we have little, we can trust God to prosper us, as long as our basic desire is to help others. In effect, this is the basic principle of stewardship, which Paul explains in 2 Corinthians 9:6-10, namely, *God will give you much so that you can give away much*:

> The point is this: the one who sows sparingly will also reap sparingly, and the one who sows bountifully will also reap bountifully. Each of you must give as you have made up your mind, not reluctantly or under compulsion, for God loves a cheerful giver. And God is able to provide you with every blessing in abundance, so that by always having enough of everything, you may

share abundantly in every good work. As it is written,
"He scatters abroad, he gives to the poor;
his righteousness endures forever."

He who supplies seed to the sower and bread for food will supply and multiply your seed for sowing and increase the harvest of your righteousness. *You will be enriched in every way for your great generosity, which will produce thanksgiving to God through us.* (emphasis mine)

A common misquotation from Scripture states that "money is the root of all evil." Paul does not say that money is the root of all evil, but rather that *"love of money* is a root of all kinds of evil" (1 Tm 6:10, emphasis mine). Love of money is the sin of avarice. The opposite is the virtue of generosity. "How does God's love abide in anyone who has the world's goods and sees a brother or sister in need and yet refuses help?" (1 Jn 3:17). By trusting God, you can afford to be generous. Trusting him to supply your needs in order to supply others' needs is simply trusting him to trust you as his emissary to share his wealth.

TWENTY-FIVE
Inadequacy and Trust

I received a humorous greeting card once that said, "You have many hidden talents. I hope somebody finds one of them some day."

Everyone has some talent, skill, ability, or charism, and God expects us to use all of our gifts to the extent that opportunities are provided. Don't bury your talents, says God's Word (see Mt 25:25). Let your light shine, but only so that God may be glorified, "and it gives light to all in the house" (Mt 5:15).

Like a family breadwinner fired from his job, the forlorn person is afflicted with a sense of inadequacy or lack of competence or self-confidence. This sometimes leads to the state of feeling bereft of God's presence, with darkness of mind and dryness in prayer. In this state of affairs, the door is opened to any number of demons, including a feeling of inferiority, discouragement, or even despair. As for so many other weaknesses to which humanity is heir, the solution lies in acquiescence to God's will and plans. By blindly trusting in God, we can be gifted with the conviction that his Spirit is dynamically at work within us in the innermost depths of our being, even when we feel inadequate to accomplish anything for him, for others, or for ourselves. By persistent faith-activated trust, we can be lifted out of the pit of negativism to absorb a portion of God's own majestic sense of worth.

TWENTY-SIX
Obedience and Trust

A pilot flying in a fog was being guided from the control tower by radar for a landing. He asked about a pole that he remembered having seen in the flight path. The flight control reply came back bluntly: "You obey *in*structions; we'll take care of *ob*structions!"

Demurring souls who hesitate to obey do not follow God's instructions and hence never learn to trust God. Souls that are not submissive are untrusting souls.

Their disobedience may take many forms, such as a refusal to tithe as the Bible requires (see Mal 3:8-10), or a refusal to love and pray for our enemies, to bless them and even do good to them (see Lk 6:27-28). Disobedient souls are not Spirit-led and may persist in the abominable practices mentioned in Galatians 5:19-21:

> Now the works of the flesh are obvious: fornication, impurity, licentiousness, idolatry, sorcery, enmities, strife, jealousy, anger, quarrels, dissensions, factions, envy, drunkenness, carousing, and things like these. I am warning you, as I warned you before: *those who do*

such things will not inherit the kingdom of God.
(emphasis mine)

That is, if we don't obey the Flight Controller, we cannot be assured of a safe landing.

If we don't obey God's Word, then we don't trust his right to require obedience of us. That means we don't trust his sovereignty or his authority over us. That, in turn, means we don't trust God himself. Are we prepared to admit that? Would we dare to state openly that we don't trust God? You can see why Paul says that such disregard of God deprives us of inheritance of his kingdom.

The paragon of trusting obedience is Jesus himself, as the author of the epistle to the Hebrews reminds us: "Jesus offered up prayers and supplications, with loud cries and tears…and he was heard because of his *reverent submission*…. He learned *obedience* from what he suffered" (Heb 5:7-8, emphasis mine).

Trustful obedience to God, regardless of our personal feelings about his rules, is ultimately trust in him to bring us to a safe landing in heaven.

TWENTY-SEVEN
Acquiescence and Trust

One of the deadliest of all poison mushrooms is the *Amanita phalloides*. For slugs and snails, however, it's a nourishing and favorite food. If that divergence of sustenance applied to humans, we'd simply say, "one man's meat is another man's poison," or, "different strokes for different folks."

Just as the divine ingenuity has immunized some animal species and not others when it comes to poisons, so also, within the human variegations, the Lord accommodates his providence to the needs of each individual and each one's calling. Some are called to be saints by their lifelong physical, mental, or emotional handicaps in a sickbed or mental institution. Others are called to become saints by a vigorous life of endurance spent in evangelizing others as missionaries, teachers, or in serving God's people as social workers, medical personnel, and so on.

The "different strokes for different folks" principle is all part of God's marvelous smorgasbord of providence. Whether a person is called to be a cloistered monk or a disease-ravaged missionary in the tropics, struggling to learn a foreign language, each is accommodating God's will and is exercising a very sanctifying acquiescence to that divine will. Implied in the sincere pursuit of these persons' callings is the trust they manifest in knowing that God is being glorified by their lives, and that his reward most certainly awaits them.

With somewhat less than theological acumen, Archie Bunker, of *All in the Family* fame, in one program was, as usual, arguing with his agnostic son-in-law (whom he affectionately called "Meathead"). Archie proclaimed with pompous certainty, "God don't make no mistakes; that's how he got to be God!"

When God doesn't explain his actions (or non-actions!), agnosticism becomes tempting as a philosophy. We tend to humanize him as one who must be making some mistake in handling this or that situation, especially when it comes to sickness, adversity, or tribulation. We may feel that we could arrange things better than God does. Yet the faith-activated trust for which we strive is the mysterious filter through which we are able to see the invisible, appreciate the ineffable, and marvel at the inscrutable in the plan of God, even when we don't understand it.

TWENTY-EIGHT

Commitment and Trust

Mythmakers of ancient England described a monster in the shape of an emaciated cow called "Chichevache" that ate nothing but faithful wives. The British let that bit of lore fade away as silly, but the Irish menfolk, who kept a tight rein on their wives, couldn't relinquish the myth that provided a bit of long-lived Irish humor. They claimed the old cow finally starved to death.

Think of the word "commitment," and then an associated word or idea. Most people respond with the phrase "fidelity in marriage," or something similar. Doubtlessly fidelity in marriage is a major commitment in our loose-moraled and uninhibited society; a disheartening percentage of married folks have never heard of, or don't want to hear, the biblical injunction that husbands and wives should "be subject to one another out of reverence for Christ" (Eph 5:21).

Yet commitment demands a far wider outreach for most people. It includes hundreds of commitments to such things as child-rearing, income-providing, giving a good example to one's children and to others, one's parish activities and its financial support, one's job, maintaining one's health, providing child support, obligations to vote, protecting the environment, and so on. One often-overlooked commitment is that of striving to "be perfect...as your heavenly Father is perfect" (Mt 5:48).

The theme of trust can hardly be defined without using the word "commitment"—or at least the basic notion. The biblical summary of the entire concept of commitment as trust in the Lord is found in the profound scriptural counsel: "Commit your way to the LORD; trust in him, and he will act" (Ps 37:5). You can't make the matter more succinct and complete than that.

TWENTY-NINE
Dependence and Trust

A fourth-grader, speaking to his teacher after religion class, observed with considerable precocity, "God's pretty smart. He put our ears in the right place long before eyeglasses were even invented."

If we were to list all the things for which we depend on

God, it would nearly exhaust our eternity! When we acknowledge our dependence on him, and do so *appreciatively*, in reference to future as well as past provisions, it is another form of the virtue of trust.

At every turn we find ourselves trusting humans, as St. John reminds us in 1 John 5:9. Yet, as he emphasizes, God is even more trustworthy. We trust barbers not to scalp, cooks not to poison, surgeons not to stab, pilots not to crash, and hunters not to use guns to murder. Though human reliability is usually very solid, it isn't perfect; but God's is. We depend on him to make the sun rise, to keep the ecology in marvelous balance, to keep the atmosphere clinging to the earth so we can breathe, to keep our hearts beating without conscious effort on our part, to keep the oceans from freezing, and to do countless other things.

The fact that he does all this is good, but he wants more than an orderly universe. He wants us humans to be awestruck by that order and to be conscious of our dependence on him because of it. In a word, he wants us to cultivate a conscious trust in recognizing our total *dependence* on him. He reminds us of this quite compellingly: "Apart from me you can do *nothing*" (Jn 15:5).

THIRTY
Influence and Trust

If you're shopping for a smile, try this one on for size. It's a ditty I fudged up during one of my more frivolous reveries:

> I have a long-stretched dachshund dog,
> who doesn't have a notion
> Of his head-to-tail delayed relay
> in showing his emotion.
> Today his mournful eyes are filled
> with tears of woe and sadness,

But his little tail keeps wagging on,
enjoying last year's gladness.

This cutesy bit of head-to-tail doggerel (pun intended) some-how reminded me of Paul's remarks to the Corinthians, stating that every part of an organism can exert an influence, delayed or not, on another part of that body. "If one member suffers, all suffer together with it; if one member is honored, all rejoice together with it" (1 Cor 12: 26). Of course, he was referring to our mutual influence as members of the mystical body of Christ. He employed the physical analogy to emphasize the interdependence and co-responsibility that we humans have for each other.

In every encounter between people, by conversation, let-ter, phone call, dining together, uniting in prayer, or whatever, there is a current of influence, often extremely subtle. This can work for good or for bad, but it is hardly ever totally neutral, even if it seems to be so. Sometimes the influence is painfully clear, as in conflictual situations, and sometimes it is delight-fully clear, as in uplifting encounters. Each encounter leaves its impress on the psyche of the participants, forming or malform-ing the personality to some degree, and, spiritually, channeling or impeding grace to each person's soul.

This interpersonal influence has multiple dimensions, including support, affirmation, love, advice, compassion, faith-building, and repentance induction. Joni Eareckson Tada, in *A Step Further*, in the midst of enormous suffering herself, writes, "One of God's purposes in increasing our trials is to sen-sitize us to people we never would have been able to relate to otherwise."

The Lord uses this dynamic, as Paul says, for:

...building up the body of Christ, until all of us come to
the unity of the faith and of the knowledge of the Son
of God, to maturity, to the measure of the full stature
of Christ.... Speaking the truth in love, we must grow

up in every way into him who is the head, into Christ,
from whom the whole body, joined and knit together
by every ligament with which it is equipped, as each
part is working properly, promotes the body's growth
in building itself up in love.

EPHESIANS 4:12-16

The ingenious providence that designed and continuously
orchestrates this interplay of human influence can be relied
upon with confidence. Our efforts to maximize the good to be
derived from human relationships imply that we are fostering
in our soul an undercurrent of trust in him to make "all things
work together for good for those who love God" (Rom 8:28).

THIRTY-ONE
Trustworthiness and Trust

During an interview, a job applicant was asked, "Do you regard
yourself as a responsible person?" He replied, "Yes, indeed. My
last boss said I was responsible for many things that happened
in the office."

The humor of this rib-tickler is based on paradoxically
opposite meanings of responsibility. The more proper meaning
is reliability, or synonymously, trustworthiness.

If you are searching for a good doctor, lawyer, financial
broker, counselor, psychiatrist, or confessor, what is the premiere quality that you look for in such a person? I'm sure your
unhesitating answer is "trustworthiness." If that quality were
missing, you would soon find yourself in great distress. To
phrase it in the quaint words of Solomon, "Like a bad tooth or
a lame foot is trust in a faithless [untrustworthy] person in time
of trouble" (Prv 25:19).

On the other hand, "A faithful envoy, healing" (Prv 13:17).
That's why God entrusted his suffering people to Moses' guidance (see Nm 12:7). Jesus held in high esteem his trustworthy

followers: "You have been trustworthy in a few things, I will put you in charge of many things" (Mt 25:21). "Whoever is faithful in a very little is faithful also in much" (Lk 16:10). (By "much" he was probably alluding to the special need for reliable persons in the end times that will require a "faithful and prudent manager...in charge of his slaves, to give them their allowance of food at the proper time" [Lk.12:42]).

For anyone who seeks to be an envoy of the Lord, reliability is an absolute requirement. "Think of us ... as stewards of God's mysteries," declared Paul. "It is required of stewards that they be found *trustworthy*" (1 Cor 4:1-2, emphasis mine).

What is especially noteworthy in Paul in this regard is his unique insight about this virtue; he always saw God as its source. His inspiring and constant dependence on God for this characteristic is remarkable: "In Christ we speak as persons of sincerity, *as persons sent from God and standing in his presence*" (2 Cor 2:17, emphasis mine). He reaffirmed this in reference to his own trustworthiness (see 2 Cor 4:2 and 1 Cor 7:25), and also in referring to his fellow "trustees," whom he complimented for this attribute: "Epaphras...a faithful minister *of Christ*" (Col 1:7, emphasis mine); "Tychicus...a faithful minister, and a fellow servant *in the Lord*" (Col 4:7, emphasis mine); "Timothy...my beloved and faithful child *in the Lord*" (1 Cor 4:17, emphasis mine). Even their work he saw as an entrustment from the Lord: "Say to Archippus, 'See that you complete the task that you have received *in the Lord*'" (Col 4:17, emphasis mine).

Reliability, according to some psychologists, is on a par with the attribute of lovability in eliciting the esteem of others. As a criterion for a happy marriage, for instance, reliability is, in the mind of many a spouse, the very touchstone of lovability. From God's point of view, at least, the two traits cannot be separated. Trust the Lord to make you trustworthy, and then enjoy the good opinion of both God and man.

THIRTY-TWO
Crises and Trust

I was transfixed, like other TV viewers, watching a child in a third-story window of a burning apartment building as the firemen in the street below were yelling for her to jump into the waiting rescue net they held. As the flames and smoke behind her grew terrifyingly close, one firefighter coaxed the little girl to jump, by yelling that the net was just like the playground trampoline on which she had played. With this, the child's hesitancy was finally overcome, and she desperately leaped into the rescue net.

In any real crisis, our motivation needs to be stimulated with extra vehemence. It's preferable to have our motivation heightened while confronting the minor day-to-day crises than it is to wait for the inevitable big crises. The practice motivation that is the easiest (and most sanctifying also) is that of trusting in the Lord to get us through it in the context of his holy will. That practice trust can be found in such things as devout reflection on the words we usually mumble unthinkingly in the Lord's Prayer: "Thy will be done."

Having survived a few rather serious California earthquakes, I've tried to renew my motivation for coping with future quakes by attempting to earthquake-proof my often-unstable trust in God. I do this by using the following scenario, replayed often in my mind, as if on a tape recorder: In any quake, I will either survive or I won't. If I do survive, then God is to be praised for preserving my life. If I don't survive, God is to be praised for starting at that time a new life for me in heaven. *Either way I win!* With this motivation, I sometimes find myself almost wishing I wouldn't survive, since I can hardly wait to get to heaven. Paradoxically, my non-survival would expedite my wish fulfillment! That may sound crazy, but it's theologically and spiritually tenable.

D-Day was perhaps the most critical day of World War II, with inclement weather, communication problems, coordination challenges, and many other difficulties. The master military engineer of that venture was General Dwight D. Eisenhower. After a period of deepest prayer, he launched the invasion, remarking to his aides before retiring for a brief rest, "Religion gives one the courage to make decisions that must be made in a crisis, but also the confidence to leave the results to a higher Power. *Only by trust in God* can anyone carrying responsibility find repose."[1]

Minor crises may be common things, like realizing that your bills are high and your bank account is low, or noticing that your gas tank is perilously near the empty mark when you are driving in a desolate area. Bigger crises are less frequent but they certainly tax our strengths, at least morally, even if not always physically. God is with you when you're shipwrecked, but in your frenzied effort to survive don't row for shore through the rocky shoals. Use your critical ingenuity to the utmost, but don't leave God out of the picture. Even battle-scathed soldiers with little or no religious convictions accepted the battlefield bromide spawned in World War II: "There's no atheist in a foxhole."

NOTE:

[1]*Encyclopedia of 7700 Illustrations* (Rockville, Md.: Assurance Publishers, 1990).

THIRTY-THREE
Godliness and Trust

A person who trusts God is a person who can be trusted. Why? Because trust gives birth to trustworthiness. Think of an unreliable person to whom you would never loan a large sum of money. Is that person really a godly person? Can you regard an untrustworthy person as one who reflects God's godliness?

The virtue of godliness is simply God-orientation. Yet we may orient ourselves toward God in many ways: by worshiping or adoring him, by thanking him, by praising him, by seeking his merciful forgiveness, and so on. Not the least of all these ways of spotlighting him in the darkness of a nearly godless world is a seemingly reckless abandonment to his supportive and protective love. This form of godliness is called trust.

Trustful reliance implies a conviction that God's Spirit is dynamically at work within us, in the innermost depths of our beings, even when we feel bereft of his presence, with darkness in our minds and dryness in our prayers. It makes us aware that everything worthwhile in God's kingdom is based on his promises, not on our feelings. It bespeaks total creatural dependence on the Creator, and hence is the one form of godliness that gives him a special divine thrill of appreciation for each trusting soul. The "God-thrill" triggered by our trust surpasses any known human experience—a unique divine reaction that he has revealed to various saints. Only in heaven will we have some grasp of how we affect God by a devout act of trust in him.

THIRTY-FOUR
God-Focus and Trust

In a teaching on the virtue of trust given at a general audience (October 23, 2002), Pope John Paul II showed how in any expression of trust in God there is an implied derivative effect; it's vetted in the cry of David in Psalm 86:11. This scriptural passage is essentially a petition for the gift of being totally God-focused; that is, the gift of single-heartedness (having undivided yearnings). In patterning our prayer after that of the psalmist, says the Pope, "every Christian…should cry out to God everywhere, while enduring trials, various temptations, and numerous scandals." We should be, he says, "like a very small child, who without ulterior motives or self-interest, *entrusts* himself fully to his father's leading as he sets out on the road of life."

Thus, the sublimated form of faith called trust is neither faith in my faith, nor faith in my prayer, but a trustful faith in a trustworthy and faithful God who will never forsake me. This kind of total trust in God's loving and gracious sovereignty is the antidote that quenches the forces of evil, sin, despair, and even the fear of death (see Ps 86:12-13 and 16:10-11).

"We often view trouble as an issue of 'me' versus 'my circumstances,'" writes Joseph Stowell in *The Upside of Down*. "In reality, hope dawns when we refocus our thinking … on the One who controls our circumstances."

Holiness is essentially union with God. As we focus on him, especially in prayer, we become more aware of that union; as we communicate with him in prayer, we start to commune with him in a communion of loving trust. While our relationship with God is diffused and not yet fully incubated by deep prayer, before the ultimate favored state is reached and sustained, we can pray only with a kind of blind, reckless abandon, "Lord, I *trust* that you are here!"

THIRTY-FIVE
Endeavors and Trust

You can easily walk on a foot-wide beam at ground level, but you may quail at the very thought of doing it one hundred stories up in a skyscraper under construction, as steeplejacks do. It isn't the width of the beam that makes it difficult; it's the height of the beam from the ground. Similarly, our outlook on many things is not objective, but contingent on circumstances.

Perfect trust in God doesn't alter our circumstances in life; it just allows us to accept those circumstances and to use them optimally for God's glory. Trust, like a tenacious vine, clings to whatever is presented to it to cling to, and when there is little support, it clings all the tighter.

Peter had a trusting faith as he walked on the water at Jesus' behest, yet when the circumstances changed, when the waves surged high, he faltered in that faith. A trusting faith enables us to walk on water, as it were; but, like Peter in his water-walking miracle, when our trusting faith weakens in the face of adverse circumstances and we find ourselves sinking in the turbulent waters that thrash around us, we should not hesitate to reach out to Jesus.

If you feel as if you are unable to do great things for the Lord because you lack talents, charisms, or sufficient education, you will tend to develop an inferiority complex. God sees you through rose-colored glasses while you see yourself through drab-gray spectacles. Using whatever talents you have—and everybody has some—set yourself to "work … while it is day; night is coming when no one can work" (Jn 9:4). Or, take to heart the words of the psalmist and make them part of your life; they promise real self-assurance to those who master the art of trusting God: "Trust in the LORD, and do good; so you will live in the land, and enjoy security" (Ps 37:3).

THIRTY-SIX
Persistence and Trust

Emblazoned on the tombstone of a hypochondriac was his pre-planned epitaph: "I *TOLD* YOU I WAS SICK!" The wit of the inscription was the fact that the poor man's persistence in his health complaints was extended beyond his demise. (He must have been gravely sick—if you'll excuse the pun.)

The persistence of trust in God that drove Paul unflinchingly onward, in spite of any impediment that lodged in his path, was the consequence of his deep-seated *conviction* of the Lord's reliability: "I am *convinced* that neither death, nor life, …nor things present, nor things to come …nor anything else in all creation, will be able to separate us from the love of God" (Rom 8:38-39, emphasis mine). For true persistence there is no force more powerful than a soul-rooted conviction. Nothing else can explain the indomitable heroism of countless martyrs who have undergone unspeakable torture for their convictions. There's no limit to a soul's persistence when its "stick-to-itiveness" derives from an underlying *conviction* that the Lord is our support (see Ps 18:18; 2 Sm 22:19).

The thicker the wall, the longer it will withstand the ravages of time—even for centuries. Likewise, the stronger the conviction of God's ever-present support, the better our endurance in withstanding the tempests of life.

THIRTY-SEVEN
Perseverance and Trust

Youngsters have become accustomed in school to engage in fire drills, and in some places earthquake drills. Yet who ever heard of end-time drills?

In the coming end times, persevering in loving trust will become critical, but also surprisingly difficult, especially in the anguish of the tribulation when God's loving concern will seem to have disappeared. Almost lamentably, Jesus asks a poignant question: "When the Son of Man comes, will he find faith on earth?" (Lk 18:8). Parables and other Scripture passages reaffirm the need for preparedness for the end times: "Be faithful until death, and I will give you the crown of life" (Rv 2:10); "You need *endurance*, so that when you have done the will of God, you may receive what was promised" (Heb 10:36, emphasis mine); "The one who endures *to the end* will be saved" (Mt 10:22; 24:13, emphasis mine).

Yet what is the stabilizing factor that enables us to stand firm? It is the Trinitarian action described by Paul (2 Cor 1:21-22): "It is God who establishes us...in Christ...and has anointed us...giving us his Spirit in our hearts." John reiterates Paul's admonition to stand firm by means of this sacred inner anointing: "The anointing that you received from him abides in you … his anointing … is true and is not a lie … abide in him (1 Jn 2:27).

From the earliest ages of the church, that anointing or infilling of the Holy Spirit was recognized as the best assurance of perseverance against the evil spirit and in dangerous times—not unlike the times in which we live today. "Only fear the LORD, and serve him faithfully with all your heart; for consider what great things he has done for you" (1 Sm 12:24).

Those who pridefully regard themselves as strong in their faith, without humbly pleading for the grace of perseverance, will find their faith—and hence their reliance on the Lord—failing in that critical time. In this regard, the words of Paul are sobering: "Keep alert, stand firm in your faith" (1 Cor 16:13). "So if you think you are standing, watch out that you do not fall" (1 Cor 10:12).

Yet now is the "acceptable time" (2 Cor 6:2); it is now, before the great tribulation, that we must cultivate a deeply formed *habit* (virtue) of trusting in God's favor—that is, his continued supporting grace to undergird and sustain our efforts to persevere. Amidst the coming carnage of the end times, our hearts must be able to cry out confidently with Job, "Though He slay me, yet will I trust Him" (Jb 13:15, NKJV).

THIRTY-EIGHT
Endurance and Trust

Endurance is simply continued exertion; it implies not just strength but sustained strength, especially for periods of extended hardship, such as prolonged illness, perhaps along with intractable pain, or prolonged unemployment, or enduring years without fulfillment, or frustration in a mediocre or unhappy marriage. From the viewpoint of eternity, this is simply a brief period of predawn darkness; as we wait for it to lift, we are confronted with another of the many tests of trust that this earthly life presents. To pass this test of our trust is simply to harbor an enduring certainty that the Sun of Justice will rise to scatter the darkness—but in his time (see Eccl 3:16).

Remember, as astronomers tell us, an eclipse of the sun never lasts more than seven and a half minutes. Endurance is easy when you know that all suffering is as brief as a blink of the eye when compared to eternity and the reward it gains for us because of our trust in the Lord and his love during that brief period. As Paul says, "I consider that the sufferings of this present time are not worth comparing with the glory about to be revealed to us" (Rom 8:18). Or, in Peter's words, "It is a credit to you if, being aware of God, you endure pain while suffering" (1 Pt 2:19).

THIRTY-NINE
Guidance and Trust

A farmer watched a bird building its nest in a heap of branches pruned from an apple tree. Having planned to clear away that pile of branches, he destroyed the unfinished nest to discourage the bird from building it there. Undaunted, the bird started building her nest again in the same spot, and again the farmer destroyed the nest. A third time the bird tried to build its nest, but this time in a rose bush near the farmhouse, where she later hatched her eggs and raised a brood of chicks—to the farmer's great delight and protective care.

While the bird had acted under blind instinct, the farmer had a long-range view of the situation and disrupted the bird's plans in order to entice it to a better plan. Like that concerned farmer, the Lord often seems to frustrate our plans as he sees the events of our lives from a much better perspective than we do. His overarching plan for us, his creatures, is called providence, which means the act of providing, and is etymologically derived from the Latin "*providere*," meaning "to see before." This is reminiscent of Jesus' words to Peter, "You do not know now what I am doing, but later you will understand" (Jn 13:7).

The Catechism of the Catholic Church (#302) reminds us that creation did not spring forth complete from the hand of the Creator, but was created *in statu viae*—"in a state of journeying" toward an ultimate perfection yet to be attained, to which God has destined it. Divine providence entails all the dispositions by which God guides his creation toward this perfection, with which we humans are called to cooperate, even when we can't see its meaning as he does. Seeing reality from God's perspective is a gift of the Holy Spirit called wisdom (see Col 1:9). Reliance on God's wisdom is the quintessential act in the art of trusting Him. In the preceding story, it was the farmer's wisdom that led the bird to accept a better outcome. That's analogous to God's trustworthy guidance of our human affairs.

A little reflection will make us aware that we spend much of our lives somewhat in the dark. We don't always know where we're going in the vicissitudes of life as we stumble down the dark alleys of the unknown. A child walking down a dark road may be terrified, wishing he had a flashlight. Yet if that child's hand is in the hand of his father as he walks along, he is even more secure than if he had a flashlight and walked alone. Isaiah 50:10 says it poignantly: "Who among you ... walks in darkness And has no light? Let him trust in the name of the Lord And rely upon his God" (NKJV). He goes on to say that those who in their attempt at self-sufficiency attempt to provide their own light "shall lie down in torment" (v. 11). Jesus, our paragon, showed us how to trust our heavenly Father. In Calvary's darkness his abandonment was inspirational: "Father, into your hands I commend my spirit" (Lk 23:46).

We are forced to make hundreds of decisions every day— some of them with serious consequences, such as choosing a marriage partner for life, or even a profession or job. Other decisions make for convenience with less meaningful after-effects, such as planning a menu for dinner, or choosing which clothing to wear. A habit of having a background trust in God on all occasions is desirable, but foreground trust is critical in making major decisions. Samuel gave his people a negative norm for choosing the right options: "Do not turn aside after useless things that cannot profit or save, for they are useless" (1 Sm 12:21). Many a life is shattered because of too much self-trust and not enough prayerful God-trust in making decisions.

In those frequent moments when you're in the dark and need guidance and feel insecure because you don't know the best way, "commit your *way* to the LORD," advises David; "*trust* in him, and he will act" (Ps 37:5). Previously, in Psalm 4:4-5, he had urged the blending of common sense with trust in God: "When you are disturbed, do not sin; ponder it…and be silent…and put your trust in the LORD." This insightful advice culminates in a prayer: "Let the light of your face shine on us, O LORD!…You alone, O LORD, make me lie down in safety" (vv. 6, 8).

FORTY
Prayer and Trust

The hallmark of Christian spirituality has always been prayer. A truly prayerful person whose prayer is based on Christian revelation can be said to be a holy person. The Lord prompted St. Faustina to encourage the use of a simple five-word prayer because it summarizes the whole of Christian spirituality: "*Jesus, I trust in you!*"

The prayer life of a truly holy person will embrace every form of prayer—adoration, praise, thanksgiving, petition, intercession, contrition, and so on. Yet each of those forms of prayer touches upon a creature-Creator relationship that implies a corresponding form of trust in that Creator. Thus, adoration implies a trust in the simple fact of one's continued dependence on God as creator and sustainer of one's very existence. Thanksgiving implies a trust in the goodness of the providence of a God who has already gifted us by providing for our needs, and our worthy desires. Petition implies a trust by way of a faith-expectancy (not always as strong as it should be) that our prayers will be granted; it encompasses at least some degree of trust that the "Ask and you shall receive" promise was not an empty one. Contrition implies a trust in God's mercy; otherwise, it would be an empty and meaningless form of remorse.

Each time you offer a prayer, even a brief outburst of praise, try to be aware of the trust element that undergirds the prayer itself and gives it meaning. Also be aware that the depth of the trust that is present in that prayer is a measure of the depth of the prayer itself.

FORTY-ONE
Striving and Trust

James Baldwin formulated one of those let-me-think-about-it aphorisms. He wrote, "Not everything that is faced can be changed, but nothing can be changed until it is faced."

Life is replete with situations that are difficult to face, from stock market meltdowns, to your child's broken leg, to finding that your car has been stolen, to being called for jury duty. You may receive an unfavorable lab report from your doctor about the cancer you had feared, or may have to make funeral arrangements for a suddenly deceased loved one. Each situation requires that we face it squarely and strive to cope with it as well as we can. Some who can't face their problems will simply panic; others will turn to alcohol, drugs, or other forms of escapism. When God is left out of the picture, he stands on the sidelines, watching us struggle without the proffered comfort, support, and guidance that we have neglected to seek.

Only the devout, trusting souls have learned to walk with the Lord through the minefield of life with the certainty that the mines that explode around them will not harm them. The more we trust in him, the easier the striving and the less unnerving the struggle will be. It was for the harried, hurried, and harassed that Psalm 91 was by God's design inserted into his holy Word. It's worth reading in full, prayerfully and frequently, if you want to master the virtue of trust in God:

You who live in the shelter of the Most High,
  who abide in the shadow of the Almighty,
will say to the LORD, "My refuge and my fortress;
  my God, in whom I trust."
For he will deliver you from the snare of the fowler
  and from the deadly pestilence;
he will cover you with his pinions,
  and under his wings you will find refuge;
  his faithfulness is a shield and buckler.
You will not fear the terror of the night,
  or the arrow that flies by day,
or the pestilence that stalks in darkness,
  or the destruction that wastes at noonday.

A thousand may fall at your side,
  ten thousand at your right hand,
  but it will not come near you.
You will only look with your eyes
  and see the punishment of the wicked.

Because you have made the LORD your refuge,
  the Most High your dwelling place,
no evil shall befall you,
  no scourge come near your tent.

For he will command his angels concerning you
  to guard you in all your ways.
On their hands they will bear you up,
  so that you will not dash your foot against a stone.
You will tread on the lion and the adder,
  the young lion and the serpent you will trample
    under foot.

Those who love me, I will deliver;
    I will protect those who know my name.
When they call to me, I will answer them;
    I will be with them in trouble,
    I will rescue them and honor them
With long life; I will satisfy them,
    and show them my salvation. (emphasis mine)

FORTY-TWO
Reliability and Trust

A seven-year-old lad was excited about being on a fishing trip with his father. At what seemed like a good area in the lake for fishing, the man stopped the boat and told his son to throw the anchor overboard. The boy promptly obeyed, only to see the anchor, along with its attached rope, sink out of sight. Only then did he sadly realize that the other end of the rope had not been attached to the boat.

From the earliest ages of Christianity, the image of an anchor in iconography, and also in Scripture, has symbolized the stabilizing influence of hope and trust. Yet the stabilizing influence of our hope-filled trust in God will not produce its intended effect if the anchor itself is not anchored—that is, firmly attached—to our very being. The anchor in itself must be reliably linked to our very soul and psyche. We must never let ourselves be detached from the other end of the anchor rope.

This rather subtle norm of spirituality may be formulated as a kind of paradox: *God relies on us to rely on him.* He is the anchor that seeks to provide the stability we desire and need, but if we become detached from him by not consistently relying on the stability that he wants to provide, then we vitiate his very desire to provide it. God is certainly reliable: "I will never leave you or forsake you" (Heb 13:5; see Dt 31:6). The question is, is our reliance on him unflagging? The keynote of reliability is constancy. Authentic trust demands reliability, expressed by a constant readiness on our part for *receiving* the constant *giving* on his part. In addition, this readiness must be so constant that it flourishes even when his giving is camouflaged as hurt.

FORTY-THREE
Humility and Trust

A politician running for office, in his attempt to elicit a vote from a neighbor lady, listed his promises of reform if he were to be elected. "You are certainly my second choice among the candidates," she said. Accepting the lukewarm compliment, the candidate asked whom her first choice was. "Anyone else who is running," she smirked.

We can safely trust in a person's promises only if we thoroughly trust that person. Every good Christian claims to trust Jesus as Lord and Savior, but many have given little thought to one of his most awesome promises—the one found in Matthew 11:29: "Take my yoke upon you, and learn from me; for I am gentle and humble in heart, and you will find rest for your souls." What is the connection between taking up a yoke and the promise of rest for one's soul?

Taking up a yoke implies a deliberate act of submission. This act enables one to "learn" Jesus' ability to be submissively humble *of heart*—interiorly, not just exteriorly—an action that provides soul rest, or inner peace, in not having to project or defend one's ego. This enigmatic statement from Jesus was a paraphrase of a teaching on receiving divine wisdom, from Sirach 6:28-30—an Old Testament deuterocanonical book: "You will find the rest she gives…a joy for you…her yoke is a golden ornament" (vv. 28-30).

When our God-given talents are humbly employed solely for his glory, not ours, then we can *trust him* to use our few loaves and fish to produce an awesome and divinely disproportionate effect in our own lives and also in others.

Trust implies the certainty that all of our talents and abilities are self-exercised but not self-engendered; they all come ultimately from the beneficent hand of God. "What do you have that you did not receive? And if you received it, why do you boast as if it were not a gift?" (1 Cor 4:7). Mary said it well: "The Mighty One has done great things for me, and holy is his name" (Lk 1:49). The double trust factor in being humble of heart is total reliance on God for his gifts, and on the assurance that they will be used for his glory, not ours.

A paradox in trusting souls who have learned to be humble of heart is the realization that the more we do for God and his people, the more we owe him for the great *privilege* of serving and glorifying him by our labor of love.

FORTY-FOUR
Petition and Trust

A four-year-old girl whose father had been absent on a military assignment overseas for two years composed an original petition while reciting her nightly prayers: "Dear God, please send me a new baby brother, so that we'll have something to surprise Daddy with when he gets home."

Not just from children, but also from adults, the Lord hears countless thousands of unseemly requests every day, as he did from his disciples James and John and their importuning mother (see Mt 20:21). To each untoward request—triggered by the "ask and you shall receive" promise—he patiently responds, "You do not know what you are asking." How would a parent answer a ten-year-old who asked for a Cadillac for Christmas? Or a toddler who wanted the freedom to play with razor blades or matches?

In an extended way I dealt with this contentious matter in my booklet and tape titled *When God Says No: Twenty-Five Reasons Why Some Prayers Are Not Answered.*[1] I have found, however, that even such in-depth teaching on this subject is not grasped by petulant petitioners who haven't learned what it means to really trust God in making their prayer petitions. They try to trust him to provide miraculous answers, but they don't trust him if the reason for the non-answer is hidden, as it is beyond their faith level to accept it as hidden.

A soul that enjoys authentic trust can accept the *righteousness* of God's apparent non-answer, even when the *reason* for the non-answer remains unknown. Yet the less-trusting soul wants to know the reason. The frustrated petitioner shows lack of true faith and trust by the very question "Why?" It is for these persons that I subtitled the booklet *"Why" Some Prayers Are Not Answered.*

Of course, *every* worthy prayer of petition is answered in some positive way (see 1 Cor 15:58), even when the good result is delayed or unrecognized. However, the more trusting the soul, the holier the person; and the holier the person, the more powerful the prayer. As St. James indicates, "The prayer of the righteous is powerful and effective" (Jas 5:16). With this subtle proviso, there is no better biblical reference to the secret of prevailing prayer than that of 1 Chronicles 5:20: "He granted their entreaty because they trusted in him."

NOTE:

[1]John H. Hampsch, *When God Says No: Twenty-Five Reasons Why Some Prayers Aren't Answered* (Huntington, Ind.: Our Sunday Visitor, 1994).

FORTY-FIVE
Gratitude and Trust

Most trail drovers of the Old West slept on open ground, amidst the cattle, but the chuck-wagon cook always slept on something soft under the protective cover of the chuck wagon itself. This was his traditional compensation for providing the cowhands with good chow. The drovers were typically grateful for the hot meals that he provided along their dusty trail.

A trusting form of gratitude does not merely trust that the Lord will provide a comforting reward for our efforts. It reaches deeper into the soul than that; it is a heartfelt thankfulness that he will, in his time, turn our stumbling blocks into stepping stones, a trusting belief that the grindstone of life will not grind us down, but polish us up.

Trust enables us to be thankful to God even when our plans have been shattered, knowing that this happened only because he has better plans for us. In relying more on the God of consolations than on the consolations of God, trust seeks the Giver more ardently than it seeks his gifts. Paul urges thanksgiving for answers to our prayers of petition, seemingly *even before* our prayers are answered: "Do not worry about anything, but in everything by prayer and supplication *with thanksgiving* let your requests be made known to God" (Phil 4:6, emphasis mine).

An even more challenging form of trust is one that is coupled with thanksgiving amidst our desolations; it's a deep, trusting faith that gives thanks to God even for upsetting things, not only after a long soul-recuperation, but *at the very moment the hardships occur.* That level of trust is not attained without much arduous and often repeated effort.

FORTY-SIX
Discouragement and Trust

Recently I saw a furniture store that sold only unfinished furniture—at reduced prices, of course, since the customers had to stain and varnish the furniture themselves. All of the customers were aware that a task awaited them in order to make the furniture usable, or at least presentable. In the sight of God, we are all in some way unfinished furniture.

Almost all serious-minded Christians, even while aware that "God's works will never be finished" (Sir 38:8), still feel disheartened by this feeling of being unfinished in many facets of their lives. But the most serious threat that discouragement proposes is in the realm of the spirit. This is consternation because of their failures to cultivate a closer relationship with God—that is, failure to grow in prayer, virtue, acceptance of his will in suffering, and so on. These souls find themselves confessing the same sins and faults time after time, with little or no sign of improvement, and often they experience not just spiritual stagnation but also backsliding. In extreme cases, such discouragement may devolve into hopelessness or out-right despair, which, Disraeli said, "is the conclusion of fools."

Under the deadening influence of discouragement, people's trust in God will also tend to shrivel up. Their self-recrimination may echo the words of the angel to the church in Ephesus: "You have abandoned the love you had at first. Remember then from what you have fallen" (Rv 2:4-5), or the angel's words to the church in Sardis: "Wake up, and strengthen what remains and is on the point of death, for I have not found your works perfect in the sight of my God" (Rv 3:2).

To the extent that their deeds are not perfect, such people feel like unfinished furniture, as it were. They need to remind themselves repeatedly to trust our Lord to finish the job—with their own cooperation, of course—for he alone is the ultimate "perfecter of our faith" (Heb 12:2). This proclivity toward dis-couragement in the face of endless fluctuations between our successes and our failures in virtue may well continue through-out our earthly struggle.

Just as a car needs periodic maintenance checkups to stay in good condition, we need periodic checkups and reconditioning—a refreshing of our former enthusiasm for things of the spirit—not once, but again and again. (An annual or semi-annual retreat may provide a structured solution.) The prob-lem of discouragement is an area where attaining and main-taining trust in Jesus as the "perfecter of our faith" is most challenging. Pray for the grace to rely on him cooperatively, not just for salvation, but also for growth in holiness.

The same difficulties that discourage a trust-weak person

will protect a more trusting soul against drooping spirits. The same sun that melts wax can harden clay. The same boiling pot that softens a potato can hard-boil an egg.

FORTY-SEVEN
Instability and Trust

I admire the unflinching courage of a blind person walking down the street with unseen dangers all around, from a steep curb to a child darting into his path. Real trust in God is often called blind trust, but what, precisely, is blind trust? It is being able, with the support of grace, which serves like a blind person's cane, to put one's total, and I mean total, full, all, everything trust in God.

Yet most of us begin by surrendering our problems to God for only a little while (or giving only certain parts of the problem to him, while hanging on to parts ourselves); then, when things don't go the way we think they should, we take back our problems. Maybe what we want doesn't come as soon as we think it should. Or maybe things are not going the way we hoped. Or maybe we try to help God along with too much of our human intervention. We're like children giving a broken toy to our father to repair, but then taking the toy back before it is repaired.

In this situation, God isn't left free to work out his magnificent plan for our lives. Our fluctuating responses reflect spiritual instability. The antidote to this instability is found in Isaiah: "Those of steadfast mind you keep in peace—in peace because they trust in you. Trust in the LORD forever, for in the LORD GOD you have an everlasting rock" (Is 26:3-4).

In the face of such instability it behooves us to recall the inspired advice of Sirach: "Trust in him, and he will help you; make your ways straight, and hope in him" (Sir 2:6). If we fluctuate in typically human instability, we can't "make our ways straight," and hence we negate any trust that we may have had before we began to vacillate in our resolve to rely on God.

Asking God for something is like using a credit card: When we ask for something, we hand over the card. As long as he has it, he can work. However, when we take it back, for whatever reason, he has to stop working and wait for us to hand back the card. In addition, when we try to help God out, it's like taking the credit card from him and jamming it into the machine the wrong way; nothing can be done until we take our hands away and let God work! Often, before he can start again, he has to fix the mess we made!

Blind trust requires us to be like a horse in a burning stable. First the horse's eyes must be covered before he can be led out safely. Sometimes God covers our eyes; he doesn't explain what's happening to us or where he is leading us. When he leads, we must blindly trust him to know what he's doing! If he were to explain it to us, it might scare us, just as the fire, if seen by the horse, would panic the animal; then we wouldn't confidently follow his leading.

God loves us and wants to help us with *all* of our problems. All we have to do is let him! Even the little problems matter to him; he wants to help! We know that God is all-powerful and all-knowing. If only we could consistently realize how much better off we would be if we put our total trust in him and let him do for us what he knows is best!

FORTY-EIGHT
Charity and Trust

The ancient Chinese had a quaint concept of hell as a banquet at which every reprobate soul had each hand glued to the end of a six-foot-long chopstick; the only way to eat was to feed each other, amidst mutual hatred. Hell is totally void of affirmation, since there's no altruism or love there, but only selfishness and hatred.

Some people pursue happiness; others create it. Opportunities to create it are all around us, since everyone is disabled to some extent; everyone needs others to exploit the full human potential. By God's providential design, we need others, not just to provide our physical and emotional needs, but also to mirror our goodness back to us by recognizing our worth and accepting and cherishing us for who we really are. Most of our unhappiness is man-made, not God-planned. Yet God's help is needed to correct the hurt of love deprivation.

The God of love who proclaimed, "I came that they may have life, and have it abundantly" (Jn 10:10) designed, as one life-giving and life-sustaining source, his own love dynamic that can operate instrumentally through us humans to provide for each other spiritual, emotional, and physical health ("fullness of life"). The giving and the receiving of this divine love as channeled through human instruments can truly add years to our lives, and life to our years.

Martin Luther King, Jr., said, "Not everybody can be famous but everybody can be great, because greatness is determined by service to others." Faith recognizes that neglect of anyone in need is neglect of Jesus himself. Our faith is empty and meaningless unless it is manifested by the loving way we relate to Jesus' vicarious presence in our fellow humans: "as you did it to...these...you did it to me" (Mt 25:40).

If any act of sincere concern for another is to be truly Christian, it must be surcharged, as Paul reminds us, with faith, hope, and love; such concern is a love that believes in a person, hopes for the best from him or her, and lovingly bears all hurts that might come from that person (see 1 Cor 13:7). Faith, "working through love" (Gal 5:6), sees Christ in each person, even "the least" of our brethren (Mt 25:40), and, with more difficulty, in those who offend us. This supernal altruism requires that we "love one another with mutual affection" and "outdo one another in showing *honor*" (Rom 12:10, emphasis mine).

It is not easy to be truly devoted to another and to honor that person *above oneself* consistently. Just think about that directive, and ask yourself honestly whether you apply it to everyone who crosses your path each day. Criticism comes easier than compliments, and it takes many compliments to offset the damage of a small bit of criticism. In his book *There's a Lot More to Health Than Not Being Sick*, Bruce Larson quips, "It takes ten 'Attaboys' to equal one 'You jerk'!" Our self-centeredness is constantly eclipsing the Christian love that we like to *think* we're practicing. It is for this reason that we must lean on God for help. Knowing of his love for each of us, we can *trust* him to help us in our efforts to spread his love.

FORTY-NINE
Rewards and Trust

Here's a thought-provoking snippet from the writings of St. John Climacus: "God in his unspeakable providence has arranged that some receive their reward for their toils even before they set to work, others while actually working, and others when their work is done, and still others only after the time of their death. Let the reader ask himself which of these four was given the opportunity of practicing the greatest trust."

If our faith is really a *personal* trusting faith, it is permeated with the last item of *doctrinal* faith listed in the Apostles' Creed: "I believe...in life everlasting." When existentially experienced, our hope-laced faith is simply trust in our divine benefactor. Like a youngster glowing with eager glee on Christmas Eve in anticipation of receiving his gifts on Christmas morning, we have no doubt that eternal bliss awaits us. Thus, trusting faith finds itself eagerly anticipating, after we survive the fleeting troubles of this life, the eternal ecstasy of heaven where we will "shout for joy," as Peter says (1 Pt 4:13). "We are confident of better things....God is not unjust; he will not overlook your work and the love that you showed for his sake" (Heb 6:9-10).

Only a callous soul would ask, "If I really trust God, what's in it for me?" The question is a bit crude, but it does deserve an answer.

In a divine response to reliant souls the Lord bestows countless graces and blessings: "Blessed are those who trust in the LORD, whose trust is the LORD" (Jer 17:7). A great reward is promised to those who consistently practice this trust: "Do not, therefore, abandon that confidence of yours; it brings a great reward" (Heb 10:35). At least part of Zophar's advice to Job emphasized the security element of the reward, even in this life: "If you direct your heart rightly, you will stretch out your hands toward him … you will be secure, and will not fear. … You will be protected and take your rest in safety" (Jb 11:13-18). The author of Proverbs restates this same advantage, but more succinctly: "One who trusts in the LORD is secure" (Prv 29:25).

A flourishing trust in Providence looks far beyond this life for safety and security; it keeps us eagerly anticipating a future reward that staggers our imagination because it is *eternal*—"an inheritance that is imperishable" (1 Pt 1:4). "God is the strength of my heart and my portion forever" (Ps 73:26).

Those who master this virtue of trusting in God as a loving Father are never disappointed: "I am the LORD; those who wait for me shall not be put to shame" (Is 49:23). Paul adds, "Hope does not disappoint us, because God's [the Father's] love has been poured into our hearts through the Holy Spirit" (Rom 5:5). To complete the Trinitarian focus, Paul says elsewhere, "Such is the confidence that we have through Christ toward God" (2 Cor 3:4). This never-disappointed confidence in the Godhead thus warrants the classical exhortation of the epistle to the Hebrews: "Let us therefore approach the throne of grace with boldness" (Heb 4:16).

While God will never disappoint *us*, we may disappoint *him*: "I have this against you, that you have abandoned the love you had at first" (Rv 2:4). His love-animated trust must not be just a sporadic or passing feeling (such as a momentary spiritual high after a sermon on this subject). Like all virtues, it must be activated and practiced consistently and perseveringly.

FIFTY

Optimism and Trust

The story is told of a faithful parishioner who, before she died, arranged to have a plastic fork in her hand when she was laid out in her coffin. Those attending her wake who inquired about this strange request found a moving mini-sermon in the explanation. During the many parish potluck suppers that she had organized, she always announced that all present should hold on to their forks after the main serving, since they would need them later for the desert. She delighted in making this announcement with a pithy bromide, which summed up her optimistic philosophy of life: "The best is yet to come!" Even as a corpse, by means of a symbolic plastic fork, she reminded the mourners to look forward to their heavenly banquet, in which "the best is yet to come."

There is always something better to look forward to, even while we anguish over the problems at hand. Certainly, "today's trouble is enough for today," as Jesus said (Mt 6:34). Yet, even the worst of the bad-hair days holds a few tiny pleasant surprises. Nevertheless, the endless day of eternity (see Rv 21:23) holds far more, and it's just around the corner. God's promises of the joys that await us in the eternal banquet should make every Christian an optimist, almost by definition. However, if we lack a deep, personal trust in the Lord, who said, "I go to prepare a place for you," then any attempt at optimism will be vacuous—a mere pie-in-the-sky fantasy.

Trust is knowing that somehow everything works together unto good for those who truly love him and lovingly strive to accept his plan (see Rom 8:28).

FIFTY-ONE

Acceptance and Trust

Some nimble-witted sage once said, "It's better to lose an argument than to lose a friend by winning an argument." Those who enter into arguments with God most frequently are those who are prone to resisting his providence when he allows adversities in their life. Biblically, Job was the pioneer of this sport, distraught as he was in his suffering.

Of course, arguing with God (usually a monologue, not a dialogue) doesn't really dissolve his friendship with us, for he will always regard us as friends, as Jesus called his disciples (see Jn 15:15). Yet humans who challenge God's plans and decisions lose something of their friendly regard for him. The arguing is usually a simple attitude of resistance to wholehearted submission to whatever he wants of us; it is a kind of non-acceptance of all the disturbing things that he permits to happen in our lives. Such non-acceptance of God's will in all circumstances is the nemesis of the virtue of trust. Nothing more effectively corrodes that virtue.

This subtly rebellious attitude has multiple consequences in our lives.

First, it is a complete waste of energy, since no one ever won an argument with the Almighty (he's the Captain of the celestial debating society!).

Second, this mutinous mentality prevents us from enjoying what we do have, as we frenetically hanker after what we don't have—a fact reminiscent of the maxim of Confucius: "Happiness does not consist in having what we want, but in wanting what we have."

Third, it blunts our eagerness for the promised blessings that come to "those who have not seen and yet have come to believe" (Jn 20:29).

Fourth, it ignores the loving concern of our heavenly Father, who "knows that you need all these things" (Mt 6:32) and exercises a hands-on control over everything—even feeding "the birds of the air" (v. 26).

Fifth, it fosters the mentality of godless persons "who strive for all these things" (v. 32).

Take careful note of one critical proviso: Total acceptance

is not total passivity in relating to God's will. That would be the heresy of Quietism, which would exclude all active obedience to God's signified will (commands and counsels), and all active *striving* for holiness. Total acceptance is to be understood as only one aspect of the Serenity Prayer: "Lord, give me the serenity *to accept what I cannot change*, and the courage to change what I can (for betterment), and the wisdom to know the difference." There is no clearer description of what is entailed in a genuine trust in God.

FIFTY-TWO
Strength and Trust

A quaint and ancient Welsh proverb states, "Three things give hardy strength: sleeping on hairy mattresses, breathing cold air, and eating dry food." Today, in our more knowledgeable age, adherence to that proverb would have very few devotees; we would find a more convincing source of "hardy strength" in a daily workout at the local gym. St. Paul would agree, although he would tack on to the advice a simple corollary: "While physical training is of some value, godliness is valuable in every way, holding promise for both the present life and the life to come" (1 Tm 4:8). He allocates to physical prowess a limited motive, and to spiritual prowess, analogously, a spiritual motive: "Athletes exercise self-control in all things; they do it to receive a perishable wreath, but we an imperishable one" (1 Cor 9:25).

For those seeking spiritual strength, the advice of St. Philip Neri is inspiring for the aspiring soul: "Cast yourself into the arms of God; be very sure that if he wants anything of you, he will fit you for the work and *find for you the necessary strength to accomplish it*." His very phrase, "cast yourself . . ." shows that he sees a relationship between trust and strength. Trust *is depending on God's strength more than our own* when we endure pain, fatigue, rejection, hardship, and toil. The strength we absorb from him is derived from the same strength that "enables him to make all things subject to himself" (Phil 3:21).

The soul that trustingly casts itself with reckless abandon into the arms of God in times of trouble and tribulation, when supernatural strength is demanded, is a soul that understands and *experiences* what Paul expressed so emphatically: "I can do all things through him who strengthens me" (Phil 4:13).

FIFTY-THREE
Serenity and Trust

While waiting my turn for a haircut in a barbershop, I watched a tiny boy squirming and screaming in fear as he experienced his first haircut. The barber had a most difficult time doing a good job in cutting the child's hair without making irregular cuts, as he carefully tried to avoid injuring the child. The father walked over to the barber chair and began to speak calmly and reassuringly to his little son. The father's quiet composure and unruffled tone of voice with loving compliments brought the child to a state of serene nonresistance—to the barber's great relief.

Like the child disturbed by the approach of the barber with scissors in his hand, we are often disturbed by imagined or even real threats in life. To attain the enviable state of true serenity in the midst of life's vicissitudes, we need to attend to the loving assurances of our heavenly Father: "Be still before the LORD, and wait patiently for him; do not fret" (Ps 37:7).

When we are disturbed by the newness of a situation, or by outright fear, it's difficult to be serene and quiet within our souls. Yet when our loving trust in him is steady, then serenity is the natural consequence, even amidst such unsettling situations. In the classic words of Richter, "How calmly may we commit ourselves to the hands of him who bears up the world!"

FIFTY-FOUR
Problems and Trust

In the midst of the stress of coping with our daily problems—
some of them overwhelming—it's difficult to apply meaningfully the words of Jesus in Matthew 11:28, telling us to come to
him when we are troubled and weary; yet it is in those very trying circumstances that he promises to give us rest and peace of
soul. He said his yoke is easy and his burden is light. Yet we
have to understand that our yoke is really his yoke if we have
truly "cast all anxiety on him" (see 1 Pt 5:7).

Try to grasp the profound significance of this Scripture-
based truth. Jesus takes *all* our burdens upon himself, and in
exchange gives us a far lesser burden and an easy yoke. When
we move the stone, as it were, to the front of the wheelbarrow,
over the wheel, it becomes easy to lift and to move; the burden
becomes easy and light.

How calm and joyful we are to be unencumbered by burdens, enjoying God's support as we rest in him, trusting him
moment by moment; we then find it easy to praise him even in
the midst of bad times, knowing that we are in his care! Instead
of spending our time stressed out by problems that seem
unsolvable, we serenely depend on him to handle those problems in his way and in his time, as long as we are doing our part
(pushing the now-easy-to-move wheelbarrow). Instead of a day
or a week or a month spent struggling with burdensome problems, that day or week or month becomes free of pressures
and light with uplifting joy. Thus, as we rejoice in the time the
Lord has given us, our mind remains open to undreamed-of
possibilities and closed to worry and futility!

After you begin to learn to trust God blindly with all your
problems, *beware*: Satan is bound to try to tell you it won't
work. He will use every trick he can think of to re-burden you
with the same problems you've just given away; he'll try to fill
your mind with worry and make you doubt that the Lord is
really concerned about your problems.

The only way to tell that you've really turned everything over to God is to determine that you are able to maintain reasonable concern, but not worry, about a problem. If you find yourself constantly thinking and talking about a problem, chances are you are still holding on to it. If you've laid everything at the feet of Jesus, there is no cause for worry! When you do this irrevocably, Satan has no ground on which to stand. When he brings it to your mind, dispel the temptation to worry by means of a moment of calming prayer. Remind yourself that the problem is now God's problem, no longer yours—it is his yoke and his burden. So if Satan tries to entice you back into the worry mode, he will need God's permission to do so—a very unlikely prospect! Anna Shipton, among her published inspiring insights, stated, "I have never committed the least matter to God that has not given me reason for limitless praise for his goodness."

Peter's experience of walking on water in the Sea of Galilee illustrates the importance of not relapsing in our trust in God when confronted with problems. Peter's miraculous walk on water at Jesus' invitation was temporarily successful. Why? Because he was walking toward Jesus, with his focus and attention on Jesus. It was only when he began to focus on the turbulent waves that he began to sink. He became preoccupied with the threatening *problem* (the surging waves) rather than remaining focused on the *problem-solver*, Jesus.

FIFTY-FIVE

Fear and Trust

Storm-chasers in Oklahoma and other parts of Tornado Alley, whether they be professionals or reckless amateurs, eagerly hope they might catch a storm on video, preferably a mighty F-5 tornado, for measuring and studying its behavior as it tears across the countryside. These storm-chasers frequently spend long periods on the road, during which time a few puffs of threatening clouds often tease them for a while and then evaporate.

As with storm chasing, so it is with much of our lives—full of dangers and uncertainties. We may not be as reckless as some amateur storm-chasers are, but we do tend to be always on the lookout for—and often actually expecting—bad things to happen. *Most* of them, of course, like hunted tornadoes, never materialize.

Quite naturally, we must face some tragedies in our lives, but true Spirit-rooted trust in God has a subtle way of eclipsing the common negatives that unnecessarily clutter our lives, such as anxiety about tomorrow, fear of illness or death, hesitation in accepting a foreseen event of divine providence, or generally fear of the unknown future. Too often our human frailty entices us to seek out human ways of coping with these threats, from installing multiple door locks to taking yoga classes. Meanwhile, our divine Counselor is urging us to rely *primarily* on him, with consummate trust, in the face of threats from things or persons: "Do not fear them," says his soothing Word, "for it is the LORD your God who fights for you" (Dt 3:22).

FIFTY-SIX

Depression and Trust

A man asked his friend on the next bar stool why he looked so sad. The depressed man said it was because he was angry with his wife, and to retaliate, she had threatened not to say a word to him for a full month.

"That should make you happy, if she irks you that much," said the friend.

"It did, but today is the last day," he groaned.

Real clinical depression is anything but humorous; it entails more than experiencing the "Monday morning blues" or some other limited period of negative feelings. Clinical depression, which involves a constellation of syndromes, is defined as a period of more than two weeks of severe emotional distress, sometimes while functionally incapacitated. It is the most common psychiatric disorder, affecting, at one time or another, approximately 15 percent of our adult population. Fortunately, there are a number of successful therapies available today for this common problem.

God witnessed what psychiatrists witness every day—the futility of trying to talk depressed persons out of their depression; they're not disposed to be uplifted from their mental misery by mere promises. The Lord commanded Moses to tell the dispirited Israelites about the Promised Land that awaited them, but to no avail: "Moses told this to the Israelites; but they would not listen to Moses, because of their broken spirit" (Ex 6:9).

Jesus, "because he himself was tested by what he suffered …is able to help those who are being tested…For we do not have a high priest who is unable to sympathize with our weaknesses, but…one who in every respect has been tested as we are" (Heb 2:18; 4:15). Thus, he was not exempt from depression at the sight of the flood of evil in the world that needed redemption. Due to his distress, "his sweat became like great drops of blood falling down on the ground" (Lk 22:44) as he anguished, "I am deeply grieved, even to death" (Mk 14:34). He found *his solace only in his trust* in the will of his Father: "Not what I want but what you want" (Mt 26:39).

A number of biblical personages were afflicted with depression, including David.

Three times David questioned himself about his own depression, arising mostly from guilt feelings and persecution. Three times he answered with the same words: "Why are you cast down, O my soul, and why are you disquieted within me? Hope in God" (Ps 42:5, 11; 43:5).

The more intractable the problem, the more there is a need for trust in the Lord to lift that crushing problem from our shoulders. Sometimes our compassionate God rewards our trust by healing through natural means such as medicine, counseling, and the like (see Sir 38); at other times he acts by his special direct and often almost miraculous intervention. We must trust him, not only for the cure, but also for his choice of the means to that cure. Furthermore, those with even deeper trust will rely on him to prevent disorders, not just to cure them.

FIFTY-SEVEN
Sickness and Trust

Fire can cook a meal, light a candle, or provide an atmosphere of coziness in a fireplace. Yet it can also destroy a house, a town, or a forest. Water can be used for sailing, swimming, brushing one's teeth, or making soup; but it can also destroy a town by a disastrous flood. Most objects, events, and forces in nature can produce either a good effect or a bad one.

The universal presence of human illness is no exception to this basic truth. Any sickness as part of God's positive will, or his permissive will, can be either a scourge or a blessing, depending on whether and how it is applied to our ultimate benefit and to God's glory. This great spiritual reality was articulated in the lengthy classical *Prayer in Time of Sickness*, by the holy scholar, Blaise Pascal. Part of that masterpiece I feel compelled to quote here:

> Thou gavest me health to serve thee, and I made a profane use of it. Thou sendest me sickness now to correct me; permit that I not use it to irritate thee by my impatience or to make a bad use of my sickness. And since the corruption of my nature is such that it renders thy favors pernicious to me, grant, O my God, that thy all-powerful grace may render my sufferings salutary. If my heart was full of affection for the worldly things while it retained its vigor, destroy that vigor for my salvation; and render me incapable of enjoying

worldly pursuits; work in me thy will, either through
weakness of my body or through giving me love for
thee, that I may enjoy but thee alone.

A trusting faith, if it is deep and grace-stimulated, finds it quite
possible, and even easy, to praise God fervently and sponta-
neously in the midst of pain, hardship, tribulation, and rejection,
or in suffering's most obvious form—sickness. Such holy trust
in God's will entails a reliance on the positive outcome of his
plan and purpose for our lives, even when his designs appear
meaningless and frustrating. The consoling words of Jeremiah
never fade from the mind of a trust-gilded soul: "I know the
plans I have for you, says the LORD, plans for your welfare and
not for harm, to give you a future with hope" (Jer 29:11).

All illness, whether physical or mental, is double-edged in
its outcome; like fire or water, it provides for us the options of
scourge or blessing. After you have employed every God-given
means to alleviate or cure the illness, then exercise the virtue of
trust to assure that it eventuates in a positive rather than a negative outcome. To consolidate your expectation of a positive
outcome, take to heart the poignant words of Romans 8:28: "We
know that all things work together for good for those who love
God, who are called according to his purpose." Accommodating
his purpose or plan for us is the essence of trust.

FIFTY-EIGHT

Bereavement and Trust

Think for a moment of one of your loved ones who has passed
away, and recall the grief you experienced at the funeral. Give
yourself a numerical score for your grief at that time, on a scale
from one to one hundred. Now think about the death of a victim of terrorism that you read about recently, and give yourself
a "grief score" for that tragic event. How do your two scores

compare? Why is there such a divergence in the grief experienced in the first as compared to the grief experienced when reading about the latter?

The answer, of course is the degree of *love* for the deceased—in one case, deep and intense, and in the other, distant and almost casual. *The greater the love, the greater the loss experienced when the beloved is taken away.* Whether the loss is that of a pet or that of a diamond ring, the pain of the loss or deprivation is always proportionate to the strength of one's affection toward the person or attachment to the object. Jesus wept at the death of his good friend Lazarus ("See how he loved him!" (Jn 11:36), even though he was dead for only four days before his miraculous resurrection.

Now take another test. How intense is your grief score today—perhaps years after the loss of a dear one—compared to your grief at the funeral? There may be surging waves of heartache periodically, but overall, we all learn that time heals all wounds (for some bereaved persons faster than for others, of course). This is God's gentle but mysterious anesthetic. "Blessed are those who mourn, for they will be comforted" (Mt 5:4).

The bereaved soul who "walks with the LORD" in the courage and trust infused by the renowned Psalm 23 walks with him through the valley of the *shadow* of death; there's no evil in a shadow—no venom in a serpent's shadow and no cutting edge in the shadow of a sword. The Good Shepherd who "has borne our infirmities and carried our diseases" (Is 53:4) leads both the dead and the mourning in the *valley* of the shadow of death. A valley is a fruitful plain; death is spiritually fruitful for the sheep dying in the arms of the Good Shepherd, as well as for the afflicted and lonely sheep bereft of their presence. The living who linger behind trust in his promise: "The LORD will be your everlasting light...and *your days of mourning shall be ended*" (Is 60:19-20, emphasis mine).

Moreover, death is a walk through this valley—a gentle,

pleasant walk. Noble Christians take delight in their pleasurable walk into the next world, stepping forward willingly as they take leave of this world, linking arms with the Master in the beautiful healing walk called death. They walk *through* this valley, never getting lost in it; they trust their great Shepherd to get them safely to the mountain of glories beyond the valley. Trust for any loved one, living or dead, is committing them totally to the Lord, without diminishing a tranquil and worry-free concern for their needs. "The people who walked in darkness have seen a great light; those who lived in a land of deep darkness—on them light has shined" (Is 9:2).

Do our beloved dead leave us, or do we leave them? They must somehow feel that we leave them if we don't paradoxically rejoice *with* them as we weep *for* them. If we truly love someone, we are happy to know that he or she is happy, even though we are sad in being deprived of his or her immediate loving presence. Yet that's where trust in God reaches its peak. For those whose trust falters under the grief of bereavement, Paul has a comforting word: "We do not want you to be uninformed, brothers and sisters, about those who have died, *so that you may not grieve as others do who have no hope* [trust]" (1 Thes 4:13, emphasis mine).

While condolences from our friends can be very helpful, ultimately only God can sustain us and dissolve our anguish. "This is my comfort in my distress, that your promise gives me life" (Ps 119:50).

FIFTY-NINE

Prudence and Trust

During World War II, an American plane, under the cloak of darkness, headed for Benghazi in North Africa. A strong tailwind accelerated the plane beyond what they felt was their air speed, so that in disbelief of their gauges they flew far beyond their destination, looking for the identifying beacon light, already far behind them. The plane finally exhausted its fuel and crashed in the desert, killing the entire crew.

Like those airmen, many a Christian has met with a disaster, not physically but spiritually, by relying on his or her personal feelings—often sincere but erroneous—rather than on the established norms of God's revealed truth, especially as they are articulated by Christ's church, "the pillar and bulwark of the truth"(1 Tm 3:15), with its Spirit-guided teaching (see Jn 16:13). Many sincere persons make what they judge to be prudent moral decisions, based only on feelings, not on divine revelation and the church's God-gifted infallibility. Those "feelings" may be contrary to Christ-imposed obedience to the church's authentic guiding authority (see Mt 18:18).

Thus, many believe in the acceptability of euthanasia, abortion, artificial birth control, cloning, premarital sex (fornication), astrology, fortune-telling, and the like. Even if these things are subjectively in accord with one's conscience, however, they are objectively sinful. Ignoring the God-assigned guides in such moral issues can lead to spiritual disasters, according to the words of Jesus: "Whoever listens to you listens to me, and whoever rejects you rejects me, and whoever rejects me rejects the one who sent me" (Lk 10:16).

These persons usually claim to be wise in their judgment, but, in the words of James, "such wisdom does not come down from above, but is earthly, unspiritual, devilish" (Jas 3:15). "Since they have rejected the word of the LORD, what wisdom is in them?" asks Jeremiah (Jer 8:9). Paul says that such false assumptions are held by persons "whose consciences are seared" (1 Tm 4:2). In Hebrews 5:13-14 it says that "the word of righteousness…is for the mature, for those whose faculties have been *trained by practice to distinguish good from evil*" (emphasis mine). James asks a challenging question about earthly wisdom as it contravenes divine wisdom: "Who is wise and understanding among you? Show by your good life that your works are done with gentleness born of wisdom" (Jas

3:13). It is pride, not humility, that can cause one's thoughts and actions to repudiate submission to legitimate authority.

When dealing with divine truths revealed directly or indirectly, so-called prudent *self-determined* decisions are based on trust in oneself, not on trust in God's guiding Spirit. "Those who trust in their own wits are fools; but those who walk in wisdom come through safely" (Prv 28:26). It was "to some who trusted in themselves that they were righteous" (Lk 18:9) that Jesus directed his scathing parable about the Publican and the Pharisee. The Lord fulminated to the prophet Ezekiel, "Though I say to the righteous that they shall surely live, yet if they trust *in their righteousness and commit iniquity,* none of their righteous deeds shall be remembered; but in the iniquity that they have committed they shall die" (Ez 33:13).

The bottom-line rationale for the immorality of one's imprudent choice or irresponsible decision is that such souls do not really *trust* what God has said about such matters, nor do they *trust* the authority he has delegated to his church. Their trust is faulty because it is misdirected. With the requisite condition of humility, this corrupted mentality can be redirected to its proper focus on the God of wisdom. The spiritual wisdom and understanding that Paul prayed for the Colossians to experience (see Col 1:9) was aimed at protecting them from spiritual disaster resulting from self-trust or human-based trust: "See to it that no one takes you captive through philosophy and empty deceit, according to human tradition, according to the elemental spirits of the universe, and not according to Christ" (Col 2:8).

SIXTY

Justice and Trust

In a town where gambling was illegal, two judges were arrested for violating that ordinance. They each agreed to preside at the other's trial. The first judge found his confrere guilty and gave him a fine of $100. Then they exchanged places as judge and defendant. The second judge also declared the other one guilty, but fined him $200. Of course, the defendant indignantly claimed that the decision was unfair, since they were equal partners in the violation. In explaining the apparent inequity, the second judge replied, "I decided on a heavier fine, since there's too much of this illegal gambling going on in this town; this is the second case like this presented to this court today!"

No one gets through this life without being victimized by injustices in one form or another, and "when they fall victim, they shall receive [only] a little help" (Dn 11:34). Not all injustices come from unjust judges like the one in Jesus' parable of Luke 18; most come from commonplace sources. Arrows of injustice are aimed at us from, among others, bankers charging hidden fees; clerks refusing refunds; shoplifters that cause inflated prices; con men; prejudiced teachers who underscore students; bosses who promote favored employees; unscrupulous auto mechanics, plumbers, or appliance repairmen; pilfering maids; duplicitous salespersons; lawyers or doctors who gouge exorbitant fees from clients or patients; inheritance-usurping relatives; burglars; reputation-corroding neighborhood gossips; and cheating spouses who shatter a marriage.

All of these, of course will have to give an exacting account of their actions to the God of justice, but that's their problem, not ours. "[But he who] trusts in the Lord…through the steadfast love of the Most High he shall not be moved" (Ps 21:7, 14). Hence, our problem as victims of injustice is striving to keep ourselves continually immersed in that "steadfast love [that] surrounds those who trust in the LORD" (Ps 32:10).

This means learning to depend on the Lord as David did when persecuted by Saul: "The LORD is my strength and my shield; in him my heart trusts; so I am helped, and my heart exults" (Ps 28:7). Being persecuted brought David to the brink of utter desperation: "Preserve my life, for I am devoted to you; save your servant who trusts in you. You are my God" (Ps 86:2).

From such a great expert in trusting we can learn that either our loving God will restore our rights or he will give us the strength to sustain the hardship resulting from the adversity, as he applies it to the glory of God and our welfare: "No good thing does the Lord withhold from those who walk uprightly" (Ps 84:11).

SIXTY-ONE
Long-Suffering and Trust

Long-suffering is an almost archaic word that sounds like a term from the outdated wordage of Shakespeare. It means, of course, putting up with a difficulty for an extended period. It's not quite the same as patience, which is basically undisturbed waiting. Long-suffering implies a bit more, namely, the lengthy sustaining of suffering or adversity.

As with all his prerogatives, God is the unchallenged champion of long-suffering—continuing in his merciful and tender love, even in the face of our sacrilegious abuse of that love. "The steadfast love of the LORD is *from everlasting to everlasting*" (Ps 103:17, emphasis mine). How much "longer" can anyone's "long"-suffering be, than "*from* everlasting (past) *to* everlasting (future)"?

Before we strive to imitate—and trust in—this celestial Master of long-suffering, let's take a moment to observe his expertise and his proficiency in this matter. Consider prayerfully these few passages from Scripture, excerpted from the many that refer to this admirable characteristic of God:

The LORD is merciful and gracious,
> *slow to anger and abounding in steadfast love.*
He will not always accuse,
> *nor will he keep his anger forever.*
He does not deal with us according to our sins,
> nor repay us according to our iniquities.
For as the heavens are high above the earth,

so great is *his steadfast love* toward those who
   fear him.

PSALM 103:8-11 (emphasis mine)

For about forty years he put up with them in the
wilderness.

ACTS 13:18

Yet he, being compassionate,
   forgave their iniquity,
   and did not destroy them;
often he restrained his anger,
   and did not stir up all his wrath.

PSALM 78:38

You are a God ready to forgive, gracious and merciful,
slow to anger and abounding in steadfast love, and you
did not forsake them.

NEHEMIAH 9:17

The Lord is … patient with you, not wanting any to
perish, but all to come to repentance.

2 PETER 3:9

The heavenly Father, through Jesus, offers to extrapolate to us
his own gracious long-suffering Spirit. This can be accomplished in two ways: *toward* us and *in* us. First, he extends long-
suffering *toward* us as he mercifully puts up with our repeated
sins and failures. Then, he extends it *in* us by giving us a share
in that marvelous divine ability to sustain our afflictions.

These afflictions that we must endure—seemingly
forever—include not only such things as months of intractable
pain, unremitting depression, or hopeless unemployment. *The
hardships that most frequently assail us come from our fellow humans*, with their unchanging foibles and endlessly irk-
some behavior. Even a miniscule share in the forbearance of
our unwearied God will enable us to put up with one another
with miraculous endurance.

This forbearance and long-suffering enables us to cope with equanimity in our dealings with inconsiderate husbands, nagging wives, obstreperous children, bad-tempered bosses, quarrelsome fellow employees, haughty pastors, and the like. Did you ever pray in similar situations for long-suffering after the model of Jesus? Note the appeal of Paul for this seldom-sought aim: "May the God of steadfastness and encouragement grant you to live in harmony with one another, in accordance with Christ Jesus" (Rom 15:5). Only a steadfast God can make us steadfast in our daily needle-prick tribulations.

It's not hard to see the need for a heroic level of trust in the Almighty to sustain us in our long-suffering. That's his work *in* us. Yet his long-suffering *toward* us is where even more trust is demanded, for this means trusting in his unflagging mercy to continue remitting our repeated sins and failures. After all, it is our very sinfulness that frustrates his work *in* us, which would provide us with long-suffering in our inter-personal problems. Ask for the twofold grace to appreciate his long-suffering mercy toward us and to sustain us in our long-suffering caused by others. Interestingly, that petition for double trust is epitomized in the Lord's Prayer: "Forgive us as we forgive..."

SIXTY-TWO

Temperance and Trust

A humpback whale releases air bubbles as it swims around a school of herring. The bubbles form a kind of fence through which the herring won't swim. The whale dives and then zooms up into the center of the tightly corralled fish, and with open mouth captures one whale of a lunch. Still, even with an oversupply of food available, the whale won't gorge itself. It consumes only what is needed for its sustenance, thus preventing the extinction of herring, but also maintaining a slim figure—slim, that is, for a whale!

Using a whale as a dieting model may seem a little bizarre, but, like most animals (except humans!) a whale eats from hunger, not from appetite. It would almost seem that the whale senses that its Creator will see to it that a food supply will always be available. Even pigs don't "pig out," as too many of us humans do when the restaurant servings are gargantuan. This built-in animal restraint, when practiced by humans, transcends a mere natural instinct; it becomes a virtue, *temperance*, one of the four cardinal virtues. It entails a Spirit-guided control that seeks not only to normalize food intake but also to avoid harmful substances like drugs, tobacco, and alcohol beyond moderation. Furthermore, it sets prudent restraints on entertainment, recreation, relaxation, and the like—all of which are proper in their rightful use. Aristotle named this virtue "eutrapelia"—a *prudent* practice of temperance.

Temperance should not be totally *self*-control; a substantial part of it must be *God*-control if it is to succeed and be constant. Paul didn't say, "I can do all things." He said, "I can do all things through him who strengthens me" (Phil 4:13). Without trusting in the Lord for "strength to be strong"—that is, strength to exert self-control consistently, you will soon be trusting only in yourself—a sure recipe for failure.

SIXTY-THREE
Wisdom and Trust

In a Christmas play, when a disingenuous kindergartner flubbed his lines he referred to the Magi as "the three Wise Guys."

Truly they must have been wise with a God-infused supernatural wisdom; somehow they were led to perceive that a newborn Baby in a distant country was the great Messiah expected from ages past. There's no explanation for a conviction so strong that with only the most meager evidence they set out on a very arduous journey. It was their divinely inspired wisdom that enabled them to *trust* that God would lead them to find this Child.

St. Thomas Aquinas says that the gift of wisdom is "sympathy for divine things"—a kind of intuition of the Lord's designs; it parallels our thinking with God's thinking, and draws us into union with him. "But anyone united to the Lord," says Paul, "becomes one spirit with him" (1 Cor 6:17).

For those with this highest sublimation of faith—the Holy Spirit's gift of wisdom (see Is 11:2)—their involvement in divine providence bespeaks both an intimate *knowledge* or familiarity with God, and an *embracing* of his plan for their lives. This double dimension—our *belief* in God as the Revealer of truth, and our *reliance* on his love-propelled plan for our welfare—is succinctly stated in 1 John 4:16: "We *know* and *rely* on the love God has for us" (NIV, emphasis mine). It engages the two highest human faculties: the mind to *know* God and his revealed truth by the virtue of faith (belief), and the will to *rely* on his providential plan by exercising the virtue of trust.

This trust or reliance on God—the second aspect of true wisdom—is the soul's devout answer to God's holy will as articulated in his loving providence. Such devout surrender to God is the soul's way of saying, "I love you too, Lord." The book of Sirach (1:4-10) reminds us that God's gift of wisdom is a participation in his own wisdom and is "poured out" upon those who love him. However, as Psalm 52:8 reminds us, *those who love him are those who trust in him.* Therefore, the awesome gift of divine insight—God's wisdom—is bestowed on those who have mastered the art of loving and trusting the Lord.

SIXTY-FOUR
Understanding and Trust

To commence means to begin. However, a commencement ceremony is a graduation—more of an end than a beginning. When you look at it, our language is filled with linguistic anomalies. We use a parkway for driving and a driveway for parking.

A cargo is moved by ship and a shipment is moved by car. Does a house burn up or burn down? A dog can smell, and if dead for a while, it smells worse! If you don't take a bath, maybe someone else will take it! You get the idea—much of our humor is derived from the double entendre in word usage.

In normal speech and writing, the only way we avoid word confusion is by the somewhat spontaneous *understanding that we derive from the context* in which the words or phrases are used. Analogous to this kind of natural understanding is a supernatural form of understanding, which provides us with a far more subtle grasp, not just of isolated words or phrases, but also of the whole sublime range of divine revelation, especially in his revealed Word, the Sacred Scriptures. It is in this theological sense that "understanding" deserves to be listed as one of the personal or sanctifying gifts of the Holy Spirit listed in Isaiah 11:2-3.

Many sincere people spend countless hours devoutly pondering the Word of God in order to enrich their souls. Nevertheless, not many of them who strive to absorb his profound truths specifically ask for the divine enlightenment and spiritual enrichment that can come only from the Holy Spirit. Only the Spirit of God can enable us to sense the deeper meaning of his revelation. To trust *only* in one's natural understanding, insights, and intuition (even with a strong theological and scriptural education) is to limit severely the reach of the human perception of the mind of God. This is how Paul describes the gift:

> These things God has revealed to us through the Spirit; for the Spirit searches everything, even the depths of God.... Now we have received not the spirit of the world, but the Spirit that is from God, so that we may understand the gifts bestowed on us by God. And we speak of these things in words not taught by human wisdom but taught by the Spirit, interpreting spiritual things to those who are spiritual. Those who are

unspiritual do not receive the gifts of God's Spirit, for they are foolishness to them, and they are *unable to understand them* because they are spiritually discerned.

1 CORINTHIANS 2:10-14, emphasis mine

For the Colossians (1:9-10), he prays that they be gifted with these powers of insight: "We have not ceased praying for you and asking that you may be filled with the knowledge of God's will in spiritual wisdom and understanding, so that you may lead lives worthy of the Lord, fully pleasing to him."

The entire thrust of these biblical passages is that we must not trust merely in our natural human minds to understand the mysteries and awesome truths hidden in the heart of God. The entire basis for the Spirit's gift of understanding is the unmeasured *trust that we must have him to supply it.*

SIXTY-FIVE

Knowledge and Trust

In a thriving business, it is said that the executive knows something about everything, the technician knows everything about something, and the switchboard operator knows everything about everything.

Of course, not even snooping operators know everything about everything—my catechism says that only God is omniscient. Moreover, his universal knowledge is not only of the "nonsnooping" type but even the nonreasoning type; it doesn't result from discursive reasoning, drawing conclusions, or even observation. It's a total, absolute, and simultaneous grasp of everything about everything in his creation, in every dimension of its reality—physical, moral, purposeful, functional, existential, and dynamic. Just acknowledging that overwhelming prerogative of his is enough to foster a deep sense of trust in his workings in us, insignificant as we seem.

Now let's put aside the microscope and use a telescope, as we peer beyond the natural gifts to the supernatural. As mentioned earlier, only the most exquisitely grace-responsive souls will receive the very special *supernatural* gifts of the Holy Spirit, as listed in Isaiah 11:2-3. St. Thomas Aquinas explains how the supernatural *Gift of Wisdom* (see chapter 63 of this book) enables the soul to appreciate the mind of God in a mystical and ethereal way. The supernatural *Gift of Understanding*, he says, is far beyond human natural understanding (see chapter 64); it enables the person to fathom, with profound insights, the deeper meanings in God's revelation, especially in his holy Word. By the supernatural *Gift of Knowledge*, teaches St. Thomas, this all-knowing God bestows a *supernatural*, transcendent share in his divine way of perceiving creatures as he intends them to relate to his will. Thus, the "God's-eye-view" of *divine things* is called wisdom, the "God's-eye-view" of his *revelation* is called understanding, and the "God's-eye-view" of *human things* is called knowledge. (An in-depth purview of these noncharismatic gifts is available in my six-hour tape, *Where Do I Go From Here?*) Endless debates rage at every turn regarding the morality or immorality of artificial contraception, abortion, homosexual practices, mercy-killing (euthanasia), "death-with-dignity" suicide, the existence of a spirit of divorce in one's home, or a spirit of addiction; the degree of compulsion in clinical pedophilia; whether a given war is morally justified, and so on. Theologians grapple with these matters with their academic expertise, using their finely honed *natural* knowledge. However, their conclusions carry a conviction that falls far below that of the soul that enjoys the *supernatural* Gift of Knowledge. For such a soul, no array of persuasive proofs is needed; with simple and overwhelming clarity and certitude, the favored soul—even if uneducated and without any theological background—*views such matters precisely as God views them*, unquestioningly and imperturbably.

The Holy Spirit of truth saturates such a person with clear judgment about what is true and what is false. Moreover, this will be grasped without even a hint of narrow-mindedness, prejudice, or bigotry. In the words of St. John, "Whoever knows God listens…and whoever is not from God does not listen…. From this we know the spirit of truth and the spirit of error" (1 Jn 4:6).

Now consider the virtue of trust in God in the context of the Gift of Knowledge. In enabling us to form sure judgments about human issues, our trust becomes as solid as the Rock of Gibraltar—not with the arrogance of a know-it-all bigot, but with a God-fused certitude as strong as the certitude of one's own existence. As Jesus stated it, "The Advocate, the Holy Spirit, whom the Father will send in my name, will teach you everything, and remind you of all that I have said to you" (Jn 14:26).

Once that gift is granted, there is boundless trust in knowing what is good and bad, what is true and false, in even the most controversial and complicated moral, ethical, and doctrinal issues. Few people have this gift, but if everyone had it, there would be no possibility for religious arguments of any kind, no need for proselytizing, no need for evangelization, no need for teaching religion, as in the end times, when "they shall all be taught by God" (see Jn 6:45; Is 54:13). What greater trust and security could we have than that?

SIXTY-SIX

Counsel and Trust

Like a self-guiding smart bomb, there is built into our human nature a divinely designed guidance system that may almost be described as a kind of self-guidance system. The Bible refers to it as "the counsel of the heart." In Sirach 37:13, for instance, it says, "Heed the counsel of your own heart, for no one is more faithful to you than it is…. Our own mind sometimes keeps us better informed than seven sentinels."

The "counsel of the heart" provides a double guidance for us in our daily lives: first, it enables us to really know ourselves, and second, it enables us to be our true selves by bringing our actions into conformity with our intentions. Thomas Merton described this double dynamic of the "counsel of the heart" when he wrote: "We cannot begin to *know* ourselves until we can see the real reasons why we do the things we do; and we cannot truly *be* ourselves until our actions correspond to our intentions that are appropriate to our own situation."[1] In other words, if you find yourself saying, "I don't know why I did that stupid thing, or made that stupid remark," then you don't really know yourself, and your actions reflect that unstable mentality.

Thus, the self-guiding smart bomb that God has implanted in our souls can thus fall away from its divinely planned trajectory. There are hundreds of New Age programs promising self-enlightenment, yet those who try them never really grow in self-knowledge. As Paul says in another context, "[They] are always being instructed and can never arrive at a knowledge of the truth" (2 Tm 3:7). This self-deception occurs in those who don't *consistently* trust in God in humility to keep their motives and ideals—and each ensuing action—in conformity with his will.

This will lead to an even deeper form of counsel, the Gift of Counsel (see Is 11:2), by which the Holy Spirit inspires us to easily choose the best means to the best end. This exquisite gift is a very advanced sublimation of the virtue of prudence; it enables us to make decisions about everything with alacrity and certainty for the most perfect choices. It operates beyond the great virtue of prudence (see Prv 8:12; Wis 8:7) but even farther above the natural skill of common sense. It affects our decisions about almost everything of importance in our lives, from job choice to determining the number of children to bring into the world, from which subject to major in for college study to the choice of a marriage partner. Imagine the trust you have in God if you have this gift!

NOTE:

[1]Thomas Merton, *No Man Is an Island* (New York: Harcourt, Brace, 1955), p. 126.

SIXTY-SEVEN
Piety and Trust

At the risk of causing my readers to suffer "quiplash," I feel that I must quote the old cliché: "The one who kneels to the Lord can stand up to anything." Or its sister truism: "The shortest distance between a problem and a solution is the distance between your knees and the floor."

Unfortunately, those humorous references to genuflectionary sanctimony might leave the impression that a prayerful posture is the ultimate criterion for piety. Of course, any prayer posture is acceptable if one's mind is on God; remember St. Dominic's twelve postures of prayer? (One Person even prayed an anguished prayer amidst a rabble mob on Calvary while hanging from a cross!)

In theological terms, piety, (or godliness) is not just facility in praying, regardless of the prayer posture. Piety is another of the gifts of the Holy Spirit—one that lets us experience a "*delight* ... in the fear of the LORD" (Is 11:3, emphasis mine). (To avoid misunderstanding of fear of the Lord, see chapter 69 of this book.) Piety is thus a delight in reverencing or worshiping God as his child; it is a gift by which we experience *a filial affection for God as our Father*, as Jesus did (see Jn 8:29).

To submit to God as our *Creator* is the virtue of religion, but to relate to him with filial affection as our *Father* is the gift of piety. This gift of filial relationship with God is bestowed upon us by the Holy Spirit: "You have received a spirit of adoption.

When we cry, 'Abba! Father!' it is that very Spirit bearing witness with our spirit that we are children of God" (Rom 8:15-16).

Thus, authentic piety is a kind of prayerful snuggling in the loving arms of our heavenly Father (try reciting the Lord's Prayer in that frame of mind). That very word picture bespeaks a warm and comfortable *trust* in our loving, protecting, providing Father. Piety goes with trust as ham goes with eggs.

SIXTY-EIGHT
Fortitude and Trust

In his book *The Screwtape Letters*, C.S. Lewis provided an interesting insight into fortitude or courage, namely, that it is exercised only at the moment it is put to the test: "It is not simply one of the virtues, but the form of every virtue at the testing point, which means at the highest point of reality. A chastity or honesty or mercy that yields to danger will be chaste or honest or merciful only on conditions. Pilate was merciful until it became risky."

President John F. Kennedy, in his *Profiles in Courage*, wrote, "Stories of past courage can teach, they can offer hope and provide inspiration. But they cannot supply the courage itself. For this, each person must look into his own soul."

I would add to that observation a remark about the finishing component of fortitude, namely, that each person must look not only *into*, but also *beyond* his own soul, *trusting in God*, who alone can supply the ultimate crucial fortitude found in true heroism, such as that of martyrs facing the burning stake. Paul provides double advice along this line: First, he says, "Keep alert, stand firm in your faith, be courageous, be strong" (1 Cor 16:13). Then, as an ultimate source of fortitude, he prescribes radical faith as reliance on God—trusting in him, not just in our "courage": "It is *God* who establishes us with you in Christ" (2 Cor 1:21, emphasis mine).

SIXTY-NINE

Fear of the Lord and Trust

Mark Twain, at a dinner party, listened silently to a lengthy discussion on heaven and hell. The hostess asked why he had been so noncommittal on the subject. "It's a matter of necessity," he replied. "I have friends in both places."

Our concern could be directed to either place (in spite of friends' location!) by the often-misunderstood biblical phrase, "fear of the Lord." If fear of the Lord is *wrongly* understood to mean *fear of punishment from the Lord*, then we would be mainly concerned with hell. If, however, fear of the Lord is *properly* understood as a *reverence* for the Lord—that is, having *a fear or dread of offending the Lord*—then our concern and focus would be on heaven (see 1 Pt 1:4). In fact, the practice of that fear, as sensitivity of conscience or reverence for him, is the most basic requirement for attaining heaven, since it is implicit in every effort to avoid sin (righteousness) or remove sin (repentance).

Every translator's nightmare is the linguistic evolution of words like "fear." To show how "fear" can be misconstrued in various contexts, consider the Word of the Lord to Jacob: "Have no fear...do not be dismayed...for I am going to save you....Have no fear...says the LORD, for I am with you" (Jer 46:27-28). Or consider its negative use by John: "There is no fear in love, but perfect love casts out fear; for fear [in its negative usage] has to do with punishment, and whoever fears has not reached perfection in love" (1 Jn 4:18). Obviously, these passages refer to the emotion of fear, not to the virtuous fear—the fear of the Lord, which in six places in the Bible is described as "the beginning of wisdom" (see, for example, Psalm 111, verse 10).

True fear of the Lord (conscience sensitivity or reverence for God) is so sublime that it is bestowed not as a mere virtue, but as a gift of the Holy Spirit. For this reason, we can say that the Lord gifts us with the very means to gift him with our reverence. The bottom line of this paradox is that we shouldn't trust only ourselves to reverence the Lord, but we should primarily trust him to inspire our reverence and worship of him. That is a dimension of trust that is seldom appreciated but easy to put into effect.

SEVENTY

Peace and Trust

A woman asked her friend how she could stay so calm in the midst of heavy pressures in her nerve-racking job. The answer was as simple as it was profound: "I'm too blessed to be stressed."

The Age of Anxiety. That's the label often attached to the turbulent, war-ravaged, terrorist-threatened time in which we live and try to survive. The experience of a deep inner peace is a rarity in our age. Even when peace of mind is attained, still peace of soul is fleeting—the supernatural peace that Jesus promised (Jn 14:27): "My peace I give to you. I do not give to you as the world gives. Do not let your hearts be troubled, and do not let them be afraid." This is what Paul refers to: "The peace of God, which surpasses all understanding, will guard your hearts and your minds in Christ Jesus" (Phil 4:7).

The ever-deepening turmoil provides a gargantuan challenge for us in seeking to cultivate an exquisitely refined faith in our Creator. This requires us to recognize that Jesus is the Alpha and Omega—"the pioneer and perfecter of our faith" (Heb 12:2). When our faith has become a truly finished or perfected faith, it becomes an imperturbable trusting conviction that God alone will have the last word on the entire world and world events. That will not occur "until the time of universal restoration that God announced long ago," as Peter proclaimed in a sermon (Acts 3:21). Until that "Day of the Lord," we must

at least try to make sense out of the chaos that shatters our ail-
ing world.

Bertrand Russell, in a humanistic revision of the scriptural
pericope "Fear of the Lord is the beginning of wisdom," said,
"*To conquer fear* is the beginning of wisdom." If his revision
was correct, however, he didn't say how to conquer fear. His
commentators felt compelled to complete this unanswered
inquiry by conjecturing that to conquer fear and attain its opposite—inner tranquility—is a matter of exercising a kind of faith
that relies on a controlling Power greater than oneself. In
Christian theology that is simply referred to as trust in God.

SEVENTY-ONE
Peacefulness and Trust

Many a sidewalk cafe in Europe charges a little extra for a
"view table." Scores of gullible tourists actually pay the extra
charge, even though every table on the sidewalk provides the
same view—nothing but passersby hurrying along the walk-
way almost within arm's reach.

There are countless peoplé, not just gullible tourists, who
are forever seeking the very best of everything that life has to
offer. These unsettled souls never seem to experience peacefulness—which is a state of mind not to be confused with the
peace described in the previous chapter. Peacefulness might
be described as the ability to find an imperturbable satisfaction
in almost any situation by a kind of ease of adaptation. This
reflects and presupposes an ability to discern what is worth
desiring, as distinguished from what are merely the useless
items of life.

St. Paul seemed to champion this simple trait: "I regard
everything as loss because of the surpassing value of knowing
Christ Jesus my Lord. For his sake I have suffered the loss of
all things, and I regard them as rubbish, in order that I may gain
Christ" (Phil 3:8).

Peacefulness is expressive of a serene trust in God as he provides in any given circumstance a design of his loving providence—a customized ambience for our specific needs, whether it be a situation of luxury or one of austerity. Our fluidity in adapting to such variegated environments is a simple exercise in the comforting virtue of trust in his providence as it relates to us personally.

SEVENTY-TWO
Possessions and Trust

One of the most heroic forms of trust is found in an unquestioning dependence on the Lord for material needs. Repeatedly this is reflected in the inspiring lives of saints committed to a spirit of poverty. Many of them, especially founders of religious groups and various charitable institutions, undertook great Spirit-inspired endeavors (not offhanded human aspirations) with an almost reckless dependence on the Lord to provide everything necessary, at just the right moment, for their God-supported plans. They signed contracts for enormous amounts of money with no cash, no credit, and no anxiety. With blissful simplicity they received "the kingdom of God as a little child" (Mk 10:15) while awaiting the downpour of material resources from God's beneficence, usually bestowed at the very deadline of absolute need. The Lord "saves the needy...so the poor have hope" (Jb 5:15).

On a lesser scale, the ancient and modern hagiographies are rife with accounts of such things as communities sitting down to dinner around an empty pot, offering thanks, and then answering a knock at the door to find a donor with an extra roasted goose or some other welcome food for which they had already said grace. I have had the privilege of personally witnessing several edifying events like this myself, among spirit-filled communities that had been gifted with the grace of unquestioning trust in the Lord.

It seems that the Lord rewards such trusting souls with need-fulfillment, but only as a teaser to remind them that their wants and not just their needs will be fulfilled in the future new age of the earth's restoration after Christ's second coming, as described by prophets like Isaiah (54:13): "Great shall be the prosperity of your children." That may have been a preview of the promised reward for those who pass Jesus' "prosperity test": "Well done, good and trustworthy slave; you have been trustworthy in a few things, I will put you in charge of many things; enter into the joy of your master" (Mt 25:21).

SEVENTY-THREE
Happiness and Trust

A craggy farmer once gave me an unsophisticated guideline for success that abounded with homespun wisdom: "Gumption," he opined, "is partly grit and partly grin." By "gumption" he meant willingness to grapple with a problem; "grit" implies determination in that effort. The "grin" is the anticipated satisfaction of accomplishment.

The personalized faith called trust—found in sincere God-seekers—has a built in "grin" as one of its authenticating characteristics. This was expounded by David as joy and delight found in every trusting soul: "Trust in the LORD...so you will live in the land, and enjoy security. Take d*elight* in the LORD, and he will give you the desires of your heart. *Commit your way to the LORD;* trust in him and he will act" (Ps 37:3-5, emphasis mine).

To delight in someone means to experience great joy and pleasure in his or her presence; this happens, of course, only if we know and love that person. To "take delight in the Lord" we must come to know him intimately and experience his fathomless love for us. This trust, as the psalm says, implies commitment, because in trusting God we commit to him all that we have—our lives, jobs, families, possessions, and so on. Our trust in him is a conviction that he will take care of us better than we could do it without his help. This kind of trust enables us to wait, in quiet joy, for him to work out what is best for us. Knowing him as a loving, caring God makes it easy to delight in him while we settle down in trustful surrender to await his inscrutable providential workings.

Yet what about God's delight in us? Certainly he delights in blessing us with answers to our prayers. Like any good father, he is delighted to see his children happy. He delights in giving gifts to us; even more, he delights in imparting *himself* to us. He wants us to realize that if we seek him and rely on him, we will find him (see Jer 29:13) and also an armload of gifts he has for us. "Strive first for... God... and all these things will be given to you as well" (Mt 6:33).

We don't have to exert much grit to get a grin, for when we trust in God he delights in making us delighted. No one could say it simpler and more pungently than the psalmist: "O LORD of hosts, happy is everyone who trusts in you" (Ps 84:12).

SEVENTY-FOUR
Expectancy and Trust

Trust includes a reliance on God's pattern and purpose for our lives, even when to us it appears meaningless, purposeless, and unattainable. Deeper levels of trust lead to an overwhelming assurance that God is the God of the future as well as the past and present; the future is in his perfect control. As long as we respond to his love for us, we need not be anxious about that future: "Do not worry about *anything*" (Phil 4:6, emphasis mine). In chapter 6 of Matthew's Gospel, Jesus repeatedly forbids us to worry (see vv. 25-34). Of course, there is a place for legitimate *concern*, such as for the spiritual welfare and future salvation of your children. Yet such concern should not entail worry or anxiety.

All worry is by its nature futuristic; no one can worry about the past (although thinking of the past may bring with it other negative emotions, like remorse, anger, and resentment). Worry is negative expectancy of the future.

Waiting for the fulfillment of God's providence is not worry; it's simply patient waiting. Yet without consummate trust, it is not easy to appreciate the mystery of God's timing in this regard, especially as it relates to his apparent delays in anticipated future events. Our expectant waiting may be waiting for answer to our prayers, or waiting for Jesus' second coming, or simply waiting to enjoy a problem-free heaven. However, such waiting has its built-in rewards: "Wait for the revealing of our Lord Jesus Christ. He will also strengthen you to the end, so that you may be blameless on the day of our Lord Jesus Christ" (1 Cor 1:7-8).

When God's unfolding providence or his answers to our prayers are delayed, he doesn't often show us why, and even *asking why* shows a certain lack of faith. It requires a rare Spirit-breathed, person-focused kind of faith—that is, trust—even to refrain from asking why. Perhaps that kind of faith deficiency explains Jesus' remark vis-à-vis faith in a futuristic context: "When the Son of Man comes, will he find faith on earth?" (Lk 18:8).

SEVENTY-FIVE
Frugality and Trust

"Backclipping" is the name given to the linguistic anomaly of amputating words. For instance, for "mathematics" we say "math," for "teenager" we say "teen," and so on. Try whiling away your time waiting at stoplights by thinking of other back-clipped words, such as exam, lab, demo, intro, tech, rehab, decaf, and the like. Why do we tend to shorten such words? It's probably more of a natural tendency toward frugality in speech than mere laziness in speech. If an abbreviated form of a word is clearly understood, after all, why use the full word? We do the same thing with the contraction. We don't (do not) hesitate to use contractions, so what's (what is) wrong with backclipping, which seems so natural?

The Lord does a lot of backclipping himself—not, of course in speech, but in his designs for our lives. This will be seen from eternity as part of his mysterious divine frugality. He may shorten the expected long life of a child killed by a reckless driver, for example; his permissive will may be his way of preventing the innocent child from growing up to meet death as a hardened unrepentant criminal. God may retrench one's job duration by an unexpected firing; he may permit a marriage to fall short of its full expected duration by permitting divorce, or claim the "death do us part" promise by bringing about early widowhood; he may curtail plans for a lifelong career by a sudden illness or incapacitation; he may shorten one's productive years by a disheartening discovery of cancer, or a forced early retirement to care for a parent with Alzheimer's disease.

"Do not boast about tomorrow," says Solomon, "for you do not know what a day may bring" (Prv 27:1). James waxes more poetic on this theme: "You do not even know what tomorrow will bring. What is your life? For you are a mist that appears for a while and then vanishes" (Jas 4:14). Whenever the Lord does any backclipping, he does it, as he does everything else, for good, not for bad. "I know the plans I have for you, says the LORD, plans for your welfare and not for harm, to give you a future with hope" (Jer 29:11).

Those who have never learned to trust the Lord to make bad situations turn out for good are those who "do not know the thoughts of the LORD; they do not understand his plan" (Mi 4:12). Even those who do trust him are often left in the dark about his plans, but they do not rebel against them; they "go with the flow" of his perfect will. Many a trusting soul has been honed into holiness by the optimism of the twenty-third psalm: "Surely goodness and mercy shall follow me all the days of my life" (Ps 23:6).

SEVENTY-SIX
Timeliness and Trust

A child's death from a ravaging illness seems to us to be outrageously premature, since in our time frame life ideally lasts into advanced adulthood. We find it hard to trust the Lord's timing when he chooses to take from this earthly garden a precious flower just beginning to bud and replant it in his heavenly garden. It will all make sense later, when we see his orchestrated plan in the celestial blueprints, from the viewpoint of the all-wise and loving God. Meanwhile, "blessed are those who have not seen and yet have come to believe" (Jn 20:29).

Faith includes knowing that God as the Lord of time wants to be the Lord of *our* time, as we strive to conform our timing to his in every event of our lives, from the timing of answers to prayer to the timing of death itself. One response of trust is the confident assurance that God's design for each of us is at this moment in the process of being fulfilled, ineluctably, whether it's unfolding swiftly or slowly. He may delay or subvert our plans when we don't *trust* enough to wait for *his* timing, or if we rebel against it.

A faith that foments trust in a timeless God is a faith that trusts him to help us to distinguish clearly between earthly time and timeless eternity, between earthly things that will enhance our eternity and those that detract from it. Ultimately, it culminates in Jesus' incisive question: "What will it profit them to gain the whole world and forfeit their life?" (Mk 8:36)

That's what happened to the Israelites six centuries before Christ. "The time has not yet come for the Lord's house to be built," claimed the selfish people who were more concerned about paneling their own houses than restoring the ruined temple of Solomon, which they had left in disarray (see Hg 1:2-4). With his own time plan disregarded, the Lord began to refer to them as "the people" rather than "my people." The covenant relationship was damaged by this lack of trust; the people hadn't yet learned to trust God's timing, but planned independently, without seeking and acquiescing to his timing. Even today most of God's people still haven't learned that lesson. In the lyrics of a popular song, "*When* will we ever learn?" For most of us, only in eternity.

SEVENTY-SEVEN
Contemplation and Trust

Oliver Cromwell, the Puritan Lord Protector of England, had his own quaint form of grace that he piously recited before each meal: "Some people have food but no appetite; some people have an appetite but no food. I have both. The Lord be praised!"

As Christians, we have a boundless supply of food for the soul in the revealed Word of God, but we may be lacking in the appetite department. Those who have learned to find the boundless source of "soul food" and who have a ravishing appetite for the spiritual nourishment that it offers are truly blessed. They see the Lord as the loving Provider and marvel at his sustained providence. Each prayerful reading or meditation on God's Word is like participating in one of those premiere events of Jesus' public life—the feeding of the multitudes with the miraculously multiplied loaves and fish. For such contemplative souls, "their delight is in the law of the LORD, and on his law they meditate day and night" (Ps 1:2).

Faith-saturated prayer in its deepest form—contemplation—penetrates God's mysteries with an inexpressible insight that faith itself cannot articulate: "On the glorious splendor of your majesty, and on your wondrous works, I will meditate" (Ps 145:5). The psalmist alludes to the ineffable soul security, and even the release of physical tension, that sustained contemplation provides: "I keep the LORD always before me; because he is at my right hand, *I shall not be moved*. Therefore my heart is glad, and my soul rejoices; *my body also rests secure*" (Ps 16:8, emphasis mine).

This resting in the embrace of the Creator elicits a trust in his love, a love that the enlightened soul recognizes and experiences as unfailing and steadfast, and hence trustworthy. This pondering looks to the past and marvels at the Lord's unfailing goodness; he is worshipped as "abounding in steadfast love" (Ps 145:8). Peering into the future, the soul anticipates God's unfailing supply of its needs, as it revels in trust and in the warmth of God's love: "We ponder your steadfast love, O God" (Ps 48:9).

The Lord has provided the spiritual food for us. If we lack the appetite, we must ask him to provide that too—and trust him to do so.

SEVENTY-EIGHT
Guilt and Trust

Someone, probably a clever TV evangelist, coined a quirky definition for the virtue of trusting in God: he calls it the "bathtub of the soul." There's nothing like a bath or shower to restore a soiled body with refreshing cleanliness; yet, a sense of absolute cleanliness of one's *soul* is even more refreshing and delightful. Of all the faces of trust (such as trust in answer to prayer, trust in his provision for one's financial security, trust in healing from the Lord, and so on), there's none more fulfilling than trusting in God's mercy to cleanse us totally from sin. That's why Jesus, in an apparition to St. Faustina, commissioned her to propagate devotion to divine mercy through the devout use of a simple and trenchant phrase: "Jesus, I trust in you." In affirming this trust in his mercy—the kind of trust Jesus responds to most eagerly—the petitioner implicitly affirms trust in all of its other expressions.

Every thinking adult, civilized or not, has a consciousness of sin, whether confessed or unconfessed. This is the quasi-universal experience of guilt (see Rom 3:23). It carries with it some intuitive dread of punishment or retribution.

In multifarious ways humankind has always attempted to cope with real or imagined guilt. People have tried self-flagellation, sleeping in coffins, spilling out their innermost humiliating secrets to psychiatrists, engaging in psychopathic masochism, starvation-like fasting, anorexia or bulimia, submitting to ceremonial crucifixion, engaging in endless hours of self-focused meditation, making arduous pilgrimages and crusades, and imagining that they're called to become hermits. The attempt to erase guilt, motivated either consciously or subconsciously, has taken literally thousands of forms over the centuries. None of these humanly engineered forms of guilt erasure has been found to be truly satisfactory. Only persons who rely trustingly on God's method of sin dissolution, as delineated in both the Old and New Testaments, have found success in this otherwise futile venture.

All sin, even that which offends our fellow humans, is ultimately an offense against God—a violation of his will as perceived (often inadequately) by the human conscience. It is therefore a rupture in a relationship between a rational (conscience-responsive) creature and its Creator. A conscience is either well formed or malformed, and consequently can either accuse or excuse any given person, as Paul states (see Rom 2:15). In its accusatory form, it operates either as prior conscience, reining us in ("Don't do that!") or posterior conscience, spawning an anguished guilt feeling ("I told you not to do that!"). In the first case we should trust God to help us avoid sin, and in the other case we should trust him to forgive us as we repent (see the next chapter in this book).

Because it is a personal relationship that is ruptured by sin, the restoration must be a very direct one-to-one *personalistic* act; after all, we can't relate personally to some impersonal or subpersonal cosmic force or entity. Divine revelation shows us that our God is a personal God, incredibly loving and merciful, and far more eager to forgive us creatures than we are eager to be forgiven. Yet he requires us to be *open* to his proffered loving forgiveness; the faith act of accepting it is precisely an act of *trust* in his mercy.

All of this makes it consummately easy, even in a flashing moment, to be relieved of all guilt. No self-scourging or other self-imposed hardships are required. It's simply a matter of surrendering to God's forgiving love, made meaningful for us by the love-motivated sufferings of his Son, Jesus. In this context, trust is the most beneficial act of personalized faith possible—it redounds to one's very salvation.

It's heartening to know that something so necessary (salvation) is something so easy. All that is necessary is a simple trust in God to manage our sins, just as we trust him to manage the supply of the air we breathe, the movement of atoms throughout the cosmos, or the rising of the sun. Of the thousands of ways of attempting to attain freedom from guilt and authentic peace, the *only* workable one is total trust in the Lord to dissolve our sins in his merciful love, like tissue paper in a blast furnace.

"If the wicked turn away from all their sins that they have committed and keep all my statutes ... none of the transgressions that they have committed shall be remembered against them....Have I any pleasure in the death of the wicked, says the LORD GOD, and not rather that they should turn from their ways and live?" (Ez 18:21-23). When one's trust is a reliance on Christ's sin-atonement, it brings about a Christ-centered peace—one that transcends any ersatz worldly tranquility: "My peace I give to you...not...as the world gives. Do not let your hearts be troubled" (Jn 14:27). The moment we stop trusting him, we are left to drown in a sea of guilt.

SEVENTY-NINE

Repentance and Trust

A store Santa Claus, trying to be kind and complimentary to a youngster, said, "I know everything about you." Yet he was taken aback by the kid's defensive response: "But, Santa, I've changed!"

Sincere change for the better is essentially an act of the will. There's no mental action more demanding of trust than the act of sincere repentance. It trusts the Lord to respond to our protestation that we've really changed—a "firm purpose of amendment" change as radical as a U-turn, which the early Greek Fathers of the church called metanoia. In this personalized repentance-forgiveness dialogue, the restoration of the relationship occurs not as the result of a mere shame or morbid remorse, but rather as a result of a "*godly* grief [which] produces a repentance that leads to salvation" (2 Cor 7:10, emphasis mine).

The Holy Scriptures mention more than five hundred times God's offer of mercy in response to our repentance; it has not only been depicted for us in New Testament parables like that of the "lost sheep," the "lost coin," and the "Prodigal Son," but also in real-life stories like the forgiveness of the woman taken in adultery, or the poignant words of the Good Thief who stole heaven from his gibbet on Calvary. And of course underscoring all this is the very real life-and-death story of the torturous atoning passion and death of Jesus.

If at any time you are crushed with guilt and need an antidote to despair in your anguish, spend a moment meditating on this one of many pertinent Scriptures alerting us to trust in God's mercy: "My little children, I am writing these things to you so that you may not sin. But if anyone does sin, we have an advocate with the Father, Jesus Christ the righteous; and he is the atoning sacrifice for our sins" (1 Jn 2: 1-2).

In view of this, we can at any time bleat out our cry for help to the Good Shepherd, asking him to disentangle us from the brambles of sin. Immediately, if our repentance is authentic by virtue of our firm purpose of amendment, we are made pure of heart, that is, soul-cleansed and assured that we are blessed: "Blessed are the pure in heart, for they will see God"

(Mt 5:8). Among other reasons, we are blessed because we are no longer subject to even *feelings* of guilt (a guilt complex). Nothing can eclipse the conviction of our restored innocence through Jesus' redeeming death (see Rom 8:35). What more satisfying form of trust could there be?

EIGHTY

Scripture and Trust

A tour guide who was showing a group of people through a steel mill astonished his listeners by saying that they could painlessly wipe their finger briefly through a small stream of glowing molten steel poured from a ladle, but only if the finger was first wet and dusted. He then asked a man in the group whether he believed that remarkable assertion, and the man affirmed that he did believe it on the basis of the guide's knowledge. Yet when the guide invited him to try it, he nervously demurred.

The guide then asked the man's wife if she would try it. With some misgivings, she did bravely pass her dusted finger through the molten steel, and was amazed to find that it was not at all painful. The guide then made a pointed observation to the husband: "You had faith in my words—you believed what I said, but your wife had more than faith. She had *trust*, because she *acted* on her belief."

When I heard about this incident, I found it reminiscent of the remark of Jesus in Matthew 7 and Luke 6, where he reproached those who call him Lord, but do not *do* what he says; they end up, he said, in a disastrous spiritual collapse for lack of a strong foundation. "Everyone who hears these words of mine and does not act on them will be like a foolish man who built his house on sand" (Mt 7:26). They truly have faith enough to hear and believe in God's revelation, but are too cowardly to act on it.

In counterpoint to such unfaithful faithful, he speaks of everyone "who hears these words of mine and acts on them."

He then describes such stalwart Christians as those who have a deep rock-based foundation for their spiritual lives. Their enriched faith in God's Word, with its laws and promises, has prepared them for the most ferocious storms of life. They are well able to withstand every negative vicissitude of life. These are the Christians whose faith has blossomed into the virtue of trust.

A wife who really trusts her husband trusts that he is telling the truth (that is, trusts his word) when he says that he is late for dinner because he had to work late. She is *certain* that he was not bedding his secretary at the local motel. If a wife knows that her husband is trustworthy, she accepts his words as trustworthy. If God is truly trustworthy—and who would deny it?—then his Word must be trustworthy.

The psalmist was unwavering in his trust of God's Word, because he trusted God who gave that Word. "I trust in your word.... My hope is in your ordinances" (Ps 119:42-43). He bemoaned his Israelite ancestors, who "believed [the Lord's] words;...but they soon forgot his works" (Ps 106:12-13). This lack of sustained trust in God's Word brought his wrath down upon his chosen people, as he told his "word transmitter," the prophet Ezekiel. The specific reason for their punishment? "My people...hear your words, but they will not obey them" (Ez 33:31).

An interesting phenomenon is that of the strong conviction that envelopes souls who ponder God's Word devoutly. They find insuperable strength, for instance, in mulling over the words of Nahum 1:7: "The LORD is good, a stronghold in a day of trouble; he protects those who take refuge in him," or the words that Peter quotes from Psalm 55:22: "Cast all your anxiety on him, because he cares for you" (1 Pt 5:7). Literally hundreds of Scripture passages offer a means of putting starch into your trust in God when it grows flaccid. In Scripture, God speaks to us. To speak back to him in a trust dialogue, try the cordial phrase premiered by the popular Mercy of God movement: "Jesus, I *trust* in you!"

In his parable of the sower and the seed, Jesus speaks of the faltering trust in his Word as exemplified by "the one who hears the word and...receives it with joy; yet such a person *has no root*...but...immediately falls away" (Mt 13:20–21, emphasis mine). Yet in his praise of a faithful and "faith-full" Christian, Jesus pithily describes sustained trust in his words as an identifying characteristic of every true Christian: "If you continue in my word, you are truly my disciples" (Jn 8:31).

If we truly trust God's Word, we will pass the most rigorous "trust test," like the woman in the steel mill tour group, and we will assiduously incorporate his words into our daily behavior. Take, for instance, his words in Luke 6:27–30: "I say to you that listen, Love your enemies, do good to those who hate you, bless those who curse you, pray for those who abuse you.... Give to everyone who begs from you; and if anyone takes away your goods [by outright theft], do not ask for them again." It's hard to find a Christian who not only believes but also lives out existentially such divine imperatives that beckon us to partake of his proffered rivers of grace. It requires consummate trust to truly live God's Word, but those who do so have found a splendid shortcut to holiness.

EIGHTY-ONE

Salvation and Trust

When we realize that we're sinners—a weakness derived from the original sin of our proto-parents, Adam and Eve—and that we're not good enough to meet God's standards, and realize how helpless we are on our own, we are given the choice to be lifted out of that bondage or to remain in it. This is a choice ultimately of accepting or rejecting the redemption that is available to us only through Christ's sacrificial death for us (see Rom 3:21-26).

In the oft-quoted words of John 3:16-17 (emphasis mine), "God so loved the world that he gave his only Son, so that everyone who *believes in him* may not perish but may have eternal life.... God did not send the Son into the world to condemn the world, but in order that the world might be saved through him." That requirement of believing in Christ means claiming him as our *Savior* (Jesus means "God who saves") as well as our *Lord*—the One to whom we agree to submit our whole lives in service and in imitation of him.

When we take this basic step into Christianity irrevocably, God sees us, not as the sinful humans that we are, but as clothed in Christ's goodness! Then, along with Jesus, God's Son, we can know that we are truly children of God with him (see Jn 1:12) and can trust him to be with us always (see Mt 28:20). The bedrock of all forms of trust in God is *total acceptance* of the gift of divine redemption—the basic Christian truth that Jesus died to save us. All other forms of trust are included in that basic one.

However, this dynamic implies a giving and a receiving: the giving or causative act (on Jesus' part) is called redemption; the other side of the coin (the receiving or acceptance of that gift on our part) is called salvation. Thus, to trust Jesus as our Redeemer is to trust that we will be saved. Notice that trust in Jesus as Redeemer is person-focused, while trust that we will be saved is doctrine-focused. The highest expression of all trust is Jesus-focused. Hence, the most encompassing act of trust that we can exercise is articulated in that popular but exquisitely simple prayer, "Jesus, I trust in you!"

EIGHTY-TWO
Self-Worth and Trust

Nutritionists like to quote the ancient adage, "You are what you eat." While it is true that our body is basically made of and sustained by what we eat, that's not the essential constituent of our being, or even of our personality. In his book *Why Am I*

Afraid to Tell You Who I Am?, John Powell says, "If I am any-thing as a person, it is what I think, judge, feel, value, honor, esteem, love, hate, fear, desire, hope for, believe in and am committed to."[1] None of these basic functions and qualities is, of course, contingent on what one eats.

Look closely at your own core values. Which do you con-sciously cultivate: compassion? loyalty? justice? honesty? If you want to know what your core values are, and hence your real self-worth, ask yourself this simple question: How would you like your family and friends to describe you to others? The answer will sharply define your core values.

Clearly each element in our value system can be cultivated by our own efforts, and further sublimated by God through his abiding presence.

Trusting God in the context of this abiding presence implies believing in God's personal love for each of us individ-ually. That divine love is perceived as more tender and intimate as our core values become more refined, and that love ranges from all eternity in the past through this present moment and into an endless future. Just knowing this makes it easy to upgrade our more noble aspirations, and this, in turn, upgrades our sense of self-worth and leads us to delight in trustfully and unhesitatingly abandoning ourselves to his embrace. Trust actively enables us to cooperate with God in his constant lov-ing desire to improve us, rather than watch us piously reproach ourselves as worthless.

NOTE:

[1]John Powell, S.J., *Why Am I Afraid to Tell You Who I Am?* (Allen, Tex.: Tabor Publishing, 1969).

EIGHTY-THREE
Fulfillment and Trust

Some of our problems are self-induced, such as a hangover from drunkenness, extra weight from gluttony, lack of agility from neglect of sufficient exercise, tax penalties because of procrastination, and so on. Other problems are caused by others: unhappiness in marriage due to lack of consideration or poor communication on the part of a spouse, deprivation due to being burglarized, traffic delays from an accident caused by a careless driver, emotional stress due to the surliness of a fellow employee, and so on.

In coping with both categories of adversity, God's marvelous providence has designed a fourfold plan for our sanctification. He is fulfilled in his desire for our complete renovation, and we find consummate fulfillment in his accomplishment of that goal. For those who trustingly submit to his providence, the Lord uses each event to sanctify them by a process of *informing, reforming, conforming*, and *transforming*. These four processes were expressed in David's prayer, couched in Psalm 143 (the so-called seventh penitential psalm). After praying for deliverance from suffering *induced by others*, he prays for divine guidance in solving *self-induced* suffering.

The core of David's plea is in verses 7-10: "Answer me quickly, O LORD; my spirit fails. Do not hide your face from me [*reforming*].... Let me hear of your steadfast love in the morning, for in you I put my trust [*conforming*]. Teach me the way I should go [*informing*], for to you I lift up my soul.... You are my God. Let your good spirit lead me [*transforming*]."

Authentic trust is the readiness to open the door immediately to Jesus when he knocks (see Rv 3:20), and to learn to hear that knock when it is a barely discernible tapping; it is to know that his whispered call expresses his gentle desire to enter more deeply into our hearts. We must trust in him boundlessly to inform, reform, conform, and transform our souls; he knows all the shortcuts to our most fulfilling fulfillment—our holiness.

EIGHTY-FOUR

Encouragement and Trust

An aspiring composer asked orchestra conductor Victor Herbert to review and play one of his amateur compositions. Seeing that it lacked merit, Herbert turned it down. Miffed, the composer retorted sardonically, "I thought you encouraged home talent."

"I do," rejoined Herbert, "but some home talent I encourage to stay at home."

Life would be heavenly if there were no discouragement, but only encouragement. The closest we can come to that state here is to become saturated with the power of the truism stated by Paul, quoting Isaiah (Rom 10:11): "No one who believes in him will be put to shame."

Some qualities are truly worth extolling, as Paul urged the Philippians (4:8): "Whatever is true, whatever is honorable, whatever is just, whatever is pure, whatever is pleasing, whatever is commendable…any excellence…anything worthy of praise." God is certainly worthy of praise, having all these qualities, but as applied to him, we don't think of praise as encouragement (except with the exuberant teen rally, "Go, go, go, God; Three cheers for God!")

Our encouragement of other humans should, of course, be enveloped in God's love: "Any encouragement in Christ, any consolation from love, any sharing in the Spirit, any compassion and sympathy" (Phil 2:1) comes ultimately from "the God of steadfastness and encouragement" (Rom 15:5). It is our duty and privilege to disseminate this God-spawned encouragement, even daily (see Heb 3:13), to "encourage one another and build up each other" (1 Thes 5:11), as exemplified by such champions of encouragement and affirmation as the Cyprian Levite, Barnabas, nicknamed "son of encouragement" (Acts 4:36; see also 11:23). We are called to be transmitters of God's support, consolation, and comforting presence to others (see 2 Cor 1:4).

Yet here's the rub: We can't transmit meaningfully what we have not received meaningfully. We must learn to receive God's loving support appreciatively to convey it to others appreciatively. The power and influence of your compliment to another will be far deeper if your own soul throbs with the loving affirmation of the Lord, "I'm so proud of you, my child, for your efforts!"

True trust in the Lord, among its other purposes, provides a reliance on him to recognize our noble efforts—and also to dissolve our less noble defects—making us ever more buoyed up by his supporting mercy and love.

EIGHTY-FIVE
Yearning and Trust

"When the gods are angry with a man, they give what he asks for." This quizzical ancient Greek proverb may have been the inspiration for Socrates' more insightful conclusion: "Our prayers should be for blessings in general, for God knows best what is good for us."

Yet even asking for blessings in general is a form of petition, and petition is the only form of prayer in which most people engage, although in actual fact the concept of prayer is far more ample than mere petition; prayer in general includes even interior actions, such as the very theme of this book—the virtue of trust. The prophet Kahlil Gibran bemoaned the typical narrowing of the life of prayer: "You pray only in distress and need; would that you would pray in the fullness of joy and in your days of abundance." The great spiritual director, Cardinal Fenelone, recommended this broad-ranged prayer: "Tell God all that is in your heart, as you would unload your heart to a friend—your pleasures and your pains, your trials and joys."

Realistically, we can't expect either prophets or theologians to enlarge the thinking of the man on the street, whose entire religious experience consists of begging his Maker to give him something; like an infant, he wants to receive but not give. So let's accommodate our discussion to that limited myopic view that sees, but can't see beyond, the "ask and you shall receive" promise of the Lord. Even an ever-yearning type of soul is gifted with multiple opportunities to grow in trust. A closer look at the issue will show why.

The first problem, says St. James, is not asking at all: "You do not have, because you do not ask" (Jas 4:2). The second problem is that, when we do ask, we may be asking for the wrong things: "You ask and do not receive, because you ask wrongly, in order to spend what you get on your pleasures" (Jas 4:3). Thus, the *what* of our request will often reflect the *why* of that request. The *why* is the motive, which may be good, bad, or neutral (which is both non-good and non-bad). All of these factors will generally determine how God responds to our requests (usually, by the way, giving preference to our *needs* over our *wishes*: "Your heavenly Father knows that you need all these things" [Mt 6:32]).

The Lord's response may be any of three possibilities: Yes, No, or Wait. If he says yes, it may be yes to our appeal, but perhaps no to our motive—as when we ask for the right thing (for example, prosperity) but for the motive of avarice or materialism; this is "asking wrongly," or "amiss" (see Jas 4:3). Conversely, he may say no to your request and yes to your ultimate motive, which he sees as good. In this case, he ignores your choice of *what* and gives you another *what*. For example, he may refuse to give you a direct cure, but may answer your prayer indirectly by guiding you to the right doctor for a cure. The exercise of trust in this type of divine response is most demanding; it's trusting God to do things his way—trusting that his way is best.

If he says yes to both the *what* and the *why*, then your answer comes just as you requested, in God's time, of course.

The exercise of trust in this situation is most rewarding and uplifting. (When the petition is for the grace of *sincere* repentance in order to receive God's forgiveness, there is never any delay.)

Yet what about the times when our yearning gets the *wait* response from the Lord? If we ourselves are not the cause of the "wait" by impediments to successful prayer, then God's teasing delay serves to sustain and thus increase our trust while it clings to him during the hold period. (See my book, *When God Says No: Twenty-Five Reasons Why Some Prayers Are Not Answered.*)

No matter which approach the Lord uses to respond to our yearnings, we are like bears in a salmon rush—the opportunities for trust are plentiful.

Our deepest yearnings of the heart, such as desires for health, prosperity, friendship, and a good job, serve an ulterior purpose beyond being opportunities for trust; they are designed by God to stimulate even deeper yearnings that reach even further, as expressed by the psalmist: "As a deer longs for flowing streams, so my soul longs for you, O God" (Ps 42:1).

EIGHTY-SIX
Joy and Trust

Leslie Weatherhead, in his book *This Is the Victory*, writes, "The opposite of joy is not sorrow. It is unbelief." That assertion is a yellow light that signals a pause for thought. It may at first sound a bit heterodox, but isn't it true that to *believe in someone unreservedly* enables you to feel comfortable with that person and even *joyful* in sharing your most intimate secrets with that person? And when the Person in whom you believe is your own personal Lord and Savior, doesn't that belief fill your soul with joy? An atheist can never experience such deep *spiritual* joy—a fruit of the Spirit, outcropping from love (see Gal 5:22); he can know only a superficial mirthfulness, jollity, or merriment.

The virtue of trust (not just the social attitude of confidence in another) is more than mere tolerance of God's providential plan for us; it's a confident reliance on the *goodness* of God to work out his will for our best interests. With Jeremiah we can exult, "The LORD is good to those who wait for him, to the soul that seeks him" (Lam 3:25). Yet every experience of another's goodness directed toward us elicits joy. Thus, the joy of receiving a thoughtful gift is an experience of the giver's goodness toward us. When God is seen as the source of any goodness directed toward us, the joy is supernal and incarnated as Christ's joy: "that my joy may be in you, and that your joy may be complete" (Jn 15:11). Trust is reliance on the Lord's ongoing goodness toward us, and that evokes a vibrant, heartfelt joy.

EIGHTY-SEVEN
Kindness and Trust

It would seem that anyone who shows consistent kindness would be easy to trust consistently. Sadly, this is not always the case. Jesus was kind to Judas, even calling him "friend" in the very act of being betrayed (see Mt 26:50). In spite of witnessing Jesus' tender kindness in healing the sick, feeding the hungry with multiplied loaves, raising the dead, and so on, Judas didn't trust him to bring about the promised final triumphant kingdom of God. Similarly, the Israelites experienced God's kindness but failed in their trust of him, as Moses lamented: "In the wilderness…you saw how the Lord your God carried you, just as one carries a child…. In spite of this, you have no trust in the Lord your God" (Dt 1:31-32).

This tragedy can happen only to those whose trust is weak or is not cultivated by an ever-deeper appreciation of the Lord's tenderhearted kindness to them. Hence the admonition of Paul: "Note then…God's kindness toward you" (Rom 11:22).

The more we appreciate and revel in the Lord's kindness to us, the more our trust in him flourishes. If I might coin a platitude: "When kindness is *exulted* trust is *exalted*."

EIGHTY-EIGHT

Gentleness and Trust

A stone tossed into a heap of wool doesn't rebound, says the proverb. Likewise, an angry remark won't rebound from a gentle soul who absorbs abuse without retaliation. Experience supports the classic axiom: "A soft answer turns away wrath, but a harsh word stirs up anger" (Prv 15:1). That is one of countless ways that Paul's basic principle is to be implemented: "Do not be overcome by evil, but overcome evil with good" (Rom 12:21). This does not preclude presenting a strong defense of the good, says Peter: "Always be ready to make your defense…yet do it with gentleness and reverence" (1 Pt 3:15-16).

Meekness, however, is not weakness. Gentleness does not exclude righteous anger or a forceful response to the evil that is to be overcome. The meek and gentle Jesus, in his triumphal palm-strewn entry into the city, fulfilled Zechariah's prophecy as one coming as "humble and riding on a donkey" (Zec 9:9); but this was the same Jesus who, hours later, irately cast the moneychangers from the temple (see Mt 21). While we forcefully confront sin, we must still love the sinner, avers St. Augustine.

Paul was often disappointed with the Corinthians, but he confronted them in the pattern of "the meekness and gentleness of Christ" (2 Cor 10:1), and urged them to likewise bear with one another "with all humility and gentleness … in love" (Eph 4:2). To the Philippians he urged, "Let your gentleness be known to everyone" (Phil 4:5). He reiterated his plea with the Colossians: "As God's chosen ones, holy and beloved, clothe yourselves with compassion, kindness, humility, meekness, and patience" (Col 3:12). The theme was so prominent in his preaching that he challenged even his disciple, Timothy, to "pursue righteousness, godliness, faith, love, endurance, gentleness" (1 Tm 6:11), "correcting opponents with gentleness" (2 Tm 2:25). To Titus he said, "Be gentle, and to show every courtesy to everyone" (Ti 3:2).

I think it was the gentle St. Francis de Sales who said, "You can catch more flies with a spoonful of honey than with a barrel of vinegar." Paul, in his guidance of the unruly Corinthians, presented them with similar alternatives: "What would you prefer? Am I to come to you with a stick, or with love in a spirit of gentleness?" (1 Cor 4:21).

Gentleness is a virtue that is not easy to attain or to maintain. Perhaps that is why it is a "fruit of the Spirit" (see Gal 5:23)—God's way of supporting human behavioral response in the uphill struggle of character building. The Almighty definitely intervened in defense of Esther: "God changed the spirit of the king to gentleness" (Est 15:8). Paul recognized the need for Spirit-power to nurture gentleness when he suggested that mature, *Spirit-filled* people with this virtue are the best ones to tackle the task of reproving delinquent persons: "My friends, if anyone is detected in a transgression, you who have received the Spirit should restore such a one in a spirit of gentleness" (Gal 6:1). James, too, suggests the Holy Spirit's role in this; "Show by your good life that your works are done with gentleness born of wisdom...the wisdom from above is...gentle" (Jas 3:13-17).

Precisely because it is difficult to be gentle consistently, we need to *trust* in the gentle Jesus in order to draw from his gentle Father the strength of his gentle Spirit upon us. If we trust ourselves to be heroically gentle, without really trusting the Lord to share his divine gentleness with us, then we must prepare to experience a disheartening and demoralizing failure!

EIGHTY-NINE
Faithfulness and Trust

Faithfulness means "to keep faith"; it is a quality, like all good qualities, that finds its counterpart in God, the prototype of all virtues. The phrase "God is faithful" occurs repeatedly in his holy Word. Yet "the one who calls you is faithful" (1 Thes 5:24), seeks to replicate that virtue in every human in all the situations of life.

One life situation, for instance, embraces our various kinds of work. Faithfulness in our assigned work, especially during times of fatigue or weariness, may require an unflagging and conscious faithful dependence on our faithful God, while not neglecting our own efforts. "Whoever serves must do so with the strength that God supplies" (1 Pt 4:11). This, of course, presupposes that we don't neglect to cooperate with that divine support. In the words of the old seamen's platitude, "Pray, sailor, but row for shore!"

Our faithfulness must be in accord with its definition, namely, that we "*keep* the faith"—that is, we don't let go of it, or don't falter in that faith in the Lord. Hence, our faithfulness requires that our dependence on him must be not only continual (uninterrupted), but also enduring (sustained endlessly).

We speak of fallen-away clergymen, fallen-away husbands or wives, or persons fallen away from the church. To be fallen away means that one has relinquished a commitment—that one is unfaithful. There would be no unfaithfulness if our faithfulness was derived from and patterned after God's. A truly faithful person is a trustworthy person, in imitation of God, who is trustworthy *because* he is faithful.

NINETY
Goodness and Trust

When we say that something is wet, precisely what do we mean? A cloth, for instance is not wet of its own nature; for it to become wet, it must be wetted by a liquid such as water. It's the liquid, not the cloth, which of its very nature is wet; the wetted cloth simply participates in the intrinsic wetness of the liquid.

In the same way, we humans are not intrinsically good in the sense of being naturally virtuous; any goodness that we have is an extrinsic participation in the intrinsic goodness of God. "The earth is full of the goodness of the Lord" (Ps 33:5, NKJV). One rather neglected way of practicing trust is to rely trustingly on God to penetrate us with his goodness, like the water-saturated cloth. David saw God's goodness, when articulated as revelation, as being reflective of his divine trustworthiness: "Your words are true, and you have promised this good thing to your servant" (2 Sm 7:28; see 1 Chr 17:26).

One of those stick-on-your-bathroom-mirror adages says: "Character is what you are; reputation is what people think you are." That's another way of saying that authentic goodness is not to be confused with popularity. One very significant sign of its authenticity is that "God's kindness [goodness] is meant to lead...to repentance" (Rom 2:4). Because of this, Paul could compliment the Roman Christians, "You yourselves are full of goodness" (Rom 15:14).

Another sign of its authenticity related to trust in God is its reliance on him to lead us through a concatenated series of consequences to our ultimate destiny. This eschatological implication of God-derived goodness has been almost poetically articulated by Charles A. Hall: "We sow our thoughts, and we reap our actions; we sow our actions and we reap our habits; we sow our habits and we reap our character; we sow our character and we reap our destiny."

A life that has been truly well lived in goodness leaves behind for others a trail of joy-filled memories and for the future a sign of a splendiferous life yet to come. When our divine Attorney assigns our bequeathal of "goods of goodness" to our progeny, let us pray that there will be a superabundance of goodness for them and others to admire and imitate for years to come.

Trust starts with appreciating the astonishing truth that by God's goodness we are made in his image and likeness. By having an immortal soul with an intellect and free will, each of us individually is greater than all animals, plants, and inanimate matter of creation put together, as St. Thomas Aquinas affirmed. That's reason for us to "celebrate…[the LORD's] abundant goodness" (Ps 145:7).

Once we are deeply aware that God's intrinsic goodness is extruded into our very human nature, our trust becomes more than a mere recognition of his creative and providential plan for us. It grows to become a reliance on him to work out that plan ultimately for our best interests. Jeremiah exulted in the truth: "The LORD is good to those who wait for him" (Lam 3:25).

NINETY-ONE
Weakness and Trust

It has been facetiously suggested that everyone should carry a highway sign around with them that says, "Under Construction." As an alternative I might suggest a more prayerful one, patterned after the plaque on my cluttered desk that reads, "Lord, Bless This Mess!" And hidden somewhere below the clutter is an acronym sign that I think of after my first hundred or so mistakes each morning; it reads: "PBP-WMGIFWMY"—which of course stands for: "Please Be Patient With Me; God Isn't Finished With Me Yet."

Less discouraging than outright sinning but perhaps even more common than sin are the simple mistakes we make on a daily basis. These mistakes include things like tactless remarks, disastrous stock market investments, misspelled words, lapses in driving skills, checking account miscalculations, lost grocery lists, spilt milk, misplaced car keys or eyeglasses, burned toast, expired driver's licenses, and empty bathroom tissue rolls.

With the psalmist, we must wonder what the faultless God really thinks of us in our failure-mottled lives. "What are human beings that you are mindful of them ... that you care for them?" (Ps 8:4). With less interrogatory and more affirmative words, Peter quotes David's advice from Psalm 55:22 regarding God's care for us: "Cast all your anxiety on him, because he cares for you" (1 Pt 5:7). Under the aegis of God's care, we must, without anxiety, truly trust him to help us somehow blunder our way to heaven, where failure is not a word in the celestial vocabulary. Yet in the process of getting there, we can do nothing more than *trust* that the Lord in his loving compassion will patiently disregard our missteps and exercise a kind of damage control—to use a political word—with the same mercy that drives him to disregard sins, once they're repented of.

Reaction to our failures and weaknesses will, of course, be as varied as any human reaction to situations. Some people take their missteps far too seriously and keep themselves in a fever of self-recrimination and self-vilification, to the point where they lose proper self-esteem, thinking that denying one's worth is only the way to holiness. Others, with a "so what?" attitude, give hardly a thought to their daily imperfections and mistakes. For those apathetic individuals who say, "Lord, you love me just the way I am," heaven echoes with the Lord's reply: "Yes, but I love you too much to leave you the way you are!"

Finally, there are those mature souls who acknowledge their weaknesses and defects with true humility and then surrender them sweetly, lovingly, and peacefully into the hands of God, in the same trust with which they expect him to keep their hearts beating while they sleep. These type of people advance daily closer to God while avoiding the pitfalls of religious recklessness on the one hand and religious masochism on the other. The closer they come to God in holiness, the more keenly they perceive their unworthiness.

Yet, as the iron of their soul trustingly rests in the divine furnace of love, it grows from warm to hot to red-hot, then white-hot, and finally molten as it is penetrated ever more deeply with the fire of his purifying love and holiness. They experience an ever-deeper meaning in the words of Jesus, "Abide in me as I abide in you" (Jn 15:4).

Trust experiences a certainty that a divine power within us is at its strongest precisely when we accept our own weakness and our utter dependence on his strength. We are humbly emboldened by "the power that also enables him to make all things subject to himself" (Phil 3:21).

Our limitless trust in God seems to satisfy him as nothing else can. That's because it corresponds to his eternal faithfulness and reliability; it honors his truthfulness; implicitly it acknowledges his divine perfections. Not to rest in God is to derail the very plan of our creaturehood. In the classic words of the *Confessions of St. Augustine*, "Our hearts are made for thee, O Lord, and they cannot find rest until they rest in thee!" (book I, chap. 1).

NINETY-TWO
Delay and Trust

Lake Vida in Antarctica is called an ice museum that preserves biological history. It has the thickest lake ice ever recorded—over fifty feet deep. Scientists from the University of Illinois recently probed to collect cores of ice from near the bottom—the oldest portion of the ice pack. The probes to that depth revealed the presence of microbes, such as cyanobacteria, frozen for the past 2,800 years! More amazing than their existence at that depth was the fact that, when those ancient frozen microbes were thawed out, they showed every sign of life by their activity and growth, as if restored by a kind of resuscitation from their twenty-eight centuries of hibernation! It's hard to imagine that those very microbes had already been there for eight centuries by the time of Christ!

It's a fanciful thought, but it would almost seem as if those billions of microbes of various species had to wait, as it were, to be resuscitated by the scientists to a renewed life. Meanwhile countless billions of other microbes are still waiting there for some possible future drastic climate change to restore them from their frozen grave to a state of growth, movement, and even reproduction. This might even provide a kind of prototype of the delay that we must endure until the time assigned for our own future bodily resurrection. Alternately, it's also reminiscent of Paul's "death-to-life" post-repentance advice: "Present yourselves to God as those who have been brought from death to life" (Rom 6:13).

The Divine Sculptor took eons to carve the Grand Canyon, and much longer to form the earth that supports the life we now enjoy. In some respects the Lord of the universe doesn't seem to be in any hurry. Yet in other respects he does show a sense of urgency in demanding prompt action on our part. For instance, he doesn't like delay in our response to his offers of grace. For emphasis, a double reference is found in Hebrews (3:7 and 3:15, quoting Psalm 95): "Today, if you hear his voice, do not harden your hearts." Certain things God wants to be accomplished *today*, that is, without delay. In such times of non-delay, faith acknowledges that God is the great "I AM"— the God of *now*, who is working right now to accomplish his purpose, at this moment and at every moment of our being, in each simple word, thought, and act of our lives.

Attuning ourselves to God's timing (see chapter 76 of this book) is a significant expression of *trusting* his sovereign will and wisdom to decide not just the *how* and the *why* of events, but also the *when*.

Typically, any delay in the fulfillment of our own plans and hopes is frustrating; the Lord also must experience a kind of divine frustration when his plans are delayed by our resistance to them. He yearns for us to trust in his wisdom that designs the proper time for the unfolding of his will. That's when we are asked to try, with trusting faith, to think with the mind of God, as it were.

Our faith, if trusting, knows that the Lord of time wants to be the Lord of *our* time, as we strive confidently to conform our timing with his in every event of our lives, from the timing of a job loss to the timing of our death, or the death of our loved ones. Especially when we are victims of a human injustice, like slander, being fired unjustly, embezzlement, or rape, justice may seem to be forever delayed. That's the time to cling to the psalmist's words: "Do not say, 'I will repay evil'; wait for the LORD, and he will help you" (Prv 20:22).

It requires trust to wait as long as God delays, but it also requires trust *not* to delay when his will is to be executed. Only with fathomless trust could Abraham *not* delay in preparing to slay his own son at God's behest.

Try to empathize, if you can, with the thinking of the God who refuses to hurry, addressed in the prayer of Moses, quoted in Psalm 90:4: "a thousand years in your sight are like yesterday when it is past, or like a watch in the night" (Ps 90:4). This is reflected in the lengthy delays between each step of salvation history: First, God "declared the gospel beforehand to Abraham" (Gal 3:8). From that time, amazingly, *he delayed 430 years* before executing the second step in that plan, the Mosaic Law (see v. 17). And then he delayed another two thousand years before implementing the third step in the plan of salvation, the epochal event of the Incarnation: "*When the fullness of time had come*, God sent his Son, born of a woman, born under the [Mosaic] law" (Gal 4:4, emphasis mine).

We're now in the midst of still another delay—a twenty-century delay so far—before the fourth step in salvation history, namely, the *parousia* or second coming of Christ, which Paul refers to as "the blessed hope and the manifestation of the glory of our great God and Savior, Jesus Christ" (Ti 2:13). For those who patiently accept this delay, yet with a holy expectancy rather than frustration, the paycheck is worth waiting for: "Christ...will appear a second time, not to deal with sin, but to save those who are eagerly waiting for him" (Heb 9:28). To reassure us of its eventuality—and thus provide a bulwark for our *trust in God*—the New Testament refers to it, directly or indirectly, 318 times!

NINETY-THREE
Confidence and Trust

Confidence and trust are almost synonymous, but not quite. Confidence usually bears the connotation of self-reliance or *self*-confidence, while trust as a supernatural virtue entails primarily a warm personal reliance on the Lord. It can be said that confidence is trust in self, while trust is confidence in God.

Faith assures us that a true love like God's is totally trustworthy, that his love is true and totally reliable. He will never forsake us, though we may forsake him. If we really trust God, we're willing to have our confidence in God put to the test to prove its genuineness and maturity. This type of trust features a quality of *readiness* for the trials of conflict, frustration, loss, or failure—all under God's guiding hand.

Yet, when fear of failure is the issue because of lack of confidence, experience shows that the soul who trusts the Lord will fail far less frequently than one who distrusts him. In the words of the saintly preacher Macduff, "Trust God where you cannot trace him. Do not try to penetrate the cloud that he brings over you; rather, look to the rainbow that is over it. The mystery is God's; the promise is yours."[1]

NOTE:

[1]Tryon Edwards, *The New Dictionary of Thoughts* (New York: Standard Book Co., 1955), p. 685.

NINETY-FOUR
Self-Confidence and Trust

A cartoon that elicited at least a gentle smirk from my otherwise stock-still face was a picture of two birds on a limb, with one wearing a packed parachute. The other was saying, "The trouble with you, Sheldon, is that you lack self-confidence." Perhaps the humor in that image is more trenchant because so many of us can identify with it.

As an epilogue to the remarks in the previous chapter, it is appropriate to explain how self-confidence is not *per se* in conflict with the virtue of trust. It is a psychologically desirable personality feature—the opposite of an inferiority complex—and it should be cultivated from the earliest childhood. This requires considerable parental guidance with a generous dose of affirmation, along with available instruments for accomplishing things and an appropriately controlled environment.

Self-confidence has to do with security in one's ability to function in society and *to accomplish works* that reflect some success or fruitfulness of one's endeavors. (Note: self-confidence should not be confused with self-esteem; for more on that quality, see the following chapter).

Self-confidence is a natural (and good) quality, but not a supernatural virtue, while trust in God is a supernatural (that is, grace-activated) virtue. *All* of one's accomplishments should be ultimately intended for God's glory—some more directly or explicitly than others, of course. When a person *trusts* the Lord to direct all these (non-sinful) accomplishments to that end, then the value of the work is enhanced and supported by God's grace. With this kind of sublimation of ordinary work, the Lord, by his creative ingenuity, can make that work long lasting in its effects, like the artistic inspiration that today is evoked by viewing ancient works of art. A highway worker may take pride in knowing that travel by car will be better, even years from now, because of his work today, but *trusting*

God to apply that remote benefit for his glory changes the human labor into a grace-filled endeavor; not so with works irrelevant to God's involvement.

Thus, any labor that makes this a better world should be both satisfying and sanctifying. It is satisfying because of self-fulfillment, but sanctifying because it is entrusted to God to make it holy, as only he can. This is the sacramental marriage or holy coupling of self-confidence and trust in God.

Of the many scriptural references to the "sanctity of labor," you might ruminate over this one for a spiritual uplift: "God is not unjust; he will not overlook your work and the love that you showed for his sake in serving the saints as you still do...Show the same diligence...to the very end...[and] inherit the promises" (Heb 6:10-12).

NINETY-FIVE
Self-Esteem and Trust

A witty but oxymoronic T-shirt quip reads: "I'm humble and proud of it."

That would be a profound theological statement, yet less witty, if it read: "I'm proud to be me, and humbled before him who made me to be me."

This counterpoint simply articulates the truth that self-esteem can be either egocentric or theocentric; that is, either prideful or humble before God.

Proper self-esteem acknowledges one's true worth, but as a God-given gift; improper self-esteem claims one's self-value, but ignores its source. "What do you have that you did not receive?" asks Paul (1 Cor 4:7). Peter tells us how to maintain our awareness of that linkage: "Humble yourselves...under the mighty hand of God" (1 Pt 5:6). The psalmist, awed by the God-given worth of each person, could easily humble himself before the Lord: "What are human beings that you are mindful of them, mortals that you care for them? Yet you have made them a little lower than God, and crowned them with glory and honor" (Ps 8:4-5).

Not too many years ago, it was a social disgrace, especially in a small, gossip-infected Tennessee town, to be known as an illegitimate child, living in a single-parent home, not knowing who or where one's father was. Such was the situation that brought a young lad, Ben Hooper, to the brink of despair with a crippling inferiority complex that resulted from his schoolmates cruelly taunting him with unrepeatable names.

One Sunday, when he was about twelve years old, he tried, as usual, to slip out of a church service just before the closing prayer, to avoid all social contact. Just as he got to the door he felt a firm hand on his shoulder, the hand of an associate minister, who glared at him menacingly as he confronted him with the question that Ben feared the most.

"Who are you, son? Whose boy are you?" the preacher asked as he studied his face intently. Then the minister broke out into a warm smile. "Wait a minute. I know who you are. I see the family resemblance. You are a child of God." With that, he slapped the lad across the rump and said, "Boy, you've got a great inheritance as a member of God's own family. Go claim it!"

That was the single most important remark in the entire life of Ben Hooper. It was the first time he had felt a real sense of worth, and it changed his life forever. He applied himself to his studies with enthusiasm and became what no one thought an illegitimate person could become—a popular governor of the state of Tennessee—and was later reelected to that same office. The big turnaround in his life was the sudden and overwhelming realization that he was loved by God as his precious child, and had been chosen by God to "inherit the kingdom" (see Mt 25:34). This truth became enormously meaningful and personally significant to him when he read the passage from Revelation 21:7: "Those who conquer will inherit these things, and I will be their God and they will be my children."

We all have that awesome inheritance, and the Lord warmly invites us, as the encouraging minister urged Ben Hooper, to "go and claim it." His invitation to us is compelling for those who know they are "his own" (Ti 2:14, for "we are children of God" (Rom 8:16), having been fashioned in "the image and reflection of God" (1 Cor 11:7), and he finds his own lovable resemblance in each one of us.

Again and again, God's Word reminds us of our real value in his eyes: "I have loved you with an everlasting love; Therefore with lovingkindness I have drawn you" (Jer 31:3 NKJV). The word "drawn" in Hebrew understanding implies a sustained close befriending love. David's plea for God to "continue your love" (see Ps 36:10) and for his love to be "steadfast" (Ps 6:4) bears the Hebrew connotation of an ongoing, ever-reliable love that is a warm, deep, and passionate—a very close and affectionate attraction of God for each of us. The depth of this parental love burgeons forth in Hosea 11:4: "I was to them like those who lift infants to their cheeks. I bent down to them and fed them." That close individualized love for each one of us, because it is infinite, exceeds our most uninhibited imagining, for only God can love infinitely. This love for you and for me continues day and night, whether we are awake or asleep, working or relaxing, praying or sinning. Who could lack self-esteem while opening himself to absorbing that kind of intimate love?

Precisely in the act of absorbing that love we are practicing the virtue of trust. That simple truth is encrusted in this morsel of food for thought: If we have trusted the Lord to make us lovable, can we not trust him to love us?

NINETY-SIX

Insecurity and Trust

The third-century bishop and martyr, St. Felix of Nola, trying to escape his persecutors, hid in a cave. Immediately a spider wove its gossamer web across the small opening, giving the appearance to his prying pursuers that the cave had not been recently occupied. When the saintly bishop later stepped out into the sunlight, he exclaimed insightfully, "Where God is, a spider's web is a wall; where he is not, a wall is but a spider's web."

Where does a fragile butterfly stay during stormy days and tempestuous nights? While rivers are surging and mountain oaks are torn from their roots, the dainty butterfly can be found clinging to the underside of a broad leaf, safe and dry. That's reminiscent of Psalm 57:1: "Be merciful to me, O God, be merciful to me, for in you my soul takes refuge; in the shadow of your wings I will take refuge, until the destroying storms pass by." That's a good prayer for insecure souls.

Animal experts who specialize in hibernation studies have found that the safer the den, the sounder the sleep. (Burglar alarm companies might find that principle useful as a sales blurb.) This bit of trivia is reminiscent of the words from Job 5:24: "You shall know that your tent is safe," or perhaps the words of David in Psalm 4:8 "I will both lie down and sleep in peace; for you alone, O LORD, make me lie down in safety." For the insecure person, in dread of terrorism, disease, accidents, and a host of other things, a good prayer for cultivating trust in God is Psalm 56:3-4: "When I am afraid, I put my trust in you.... What can flesh do to me?"

All of us, especially insecure souls, need to remind ourselves to reactivate frequently our trust in the loving God who is watching over us day and night. Any time you need a scriptural meditation on this great reality, open your Bible to Psalm 139 and read it prayerfully. You'll breathe a lot easier, I assure you.

NINETY-SEVEN
God-Sovereignty and Trust

There are two kinds of atheists: cogitative and ethical. The first type strives to prove his position by denying a need for any deity, while the second type cannot accept a God who sets rules of morality. The first type seeks assurance from his intellect, while the second type seeks assurance from the drives of his will; "By their wickedness [they] suppress the truth," Paul says (Rom 1:18).

Both types of atheism challenge the need or desire for any divine sovereignty. Speaking of these godless thinkers, Paul says, "What can be known about God is plain to them, because God has shown it to them. Ever since the creation of the world his eternal power and divine nature, invisible though they are, have been understood and seen through the things he has made. So they are without excuse...they became futile in their thinking, and their senseless minds were darkened" (vv. 19-21).

In his general audience of October 23, 2002, Pope John Paul II, commenting on Psalm 86, reminded his listeners that both space and time—the full reach of the universe and the full reach of history—give ample witness to God's absolute sovereignty. The immediate corollary of this truth, said the Pope, is the conviction that "Only God, upon whom we creatures depend and to whom we all must turn in an attitude of adoration, can offer complete deliverance." This, of course, does not mean that we are free to disregard normal prudent means to live a full, safe, and holy life. It means that our every human decision is placed under the purview of his loving and dependable control and protection.

Since this God is not an aloof deity who is uninterested in his creatures—he's not just "a" God or "the" God, but "my" God—we should, like David, cry out to him in a trust-filled plea: "Save your servant who *trusts* in you. You are *my* God" (Ps 86:2, emphasis mine). Our limited and prejudicial thinking tends to regard the God of sovereign majesty as a God lacking any personalism. We tend to believe life's events are happenstance rather than divine providence.

What conditions would you stipulate in order to allow someone to be totally in charge of your life—that is, to exert complete sovereignty over your existence, status, health, prosperity, and so on? Probably you would require that such a person have such qualities as perfect wisdom, complete objectivity, and enormous power. A sovereign person would have to be able to see the end as perfectly as the beginning, be unprejudiced, and entertain no fears, limitations, or ignorance. He would have to always know what is best for you, diligently and consistently pursue that goal, never make a mistake, bring everything to a perfect conclusion with unshakable confidence in himself, and above all, have a deep concern for your welfare, with boundless love for you. Who besides God would qualify for this challenge?

Under the sovereignty of such a God, we can easily follow St. Augustine's advice: "Leave the past to the mercy of God, the present to the love of God, and the future to the sovereign providence of God." The result for us will be an increase in confidence, a decrease in insecurity, a vanishing of worry, and an imperturbable tranquility. It behooves us to pray often for the gift of a deep and unrelenting *personal* trust in this very *personal* but sovereign God.

NINETY-EIGHT
Fruitfulness and Trust

In 1890, when a St. Louis gerontologist puréed peanuts for easy digestion by his elderly patients, he never dreamed that his prescribed "peanut butter" would grow into the billion-dollar business that it is today. Often our limited prospects are not only fulfilled but even exceeded. Even when we lack foresight and expectancy, God can still transform our little acorn into a mighty oak tree.

Yet a higher level of trust is exercised when our efforts are replete with unquestioned expectancy. We expect, among other things, that God will use our few loaves and fishes to produce a divinely disproportionate effect in our lives and in those we encounter; that disproportionate effect is called "the hundredfold."

If you'd like to ponder an aspect of trust that will lift your spirits, just consider Paul's uplifting reminder about the fruitfulness of our efforts for God's glory. He reminds us that nothing we do for the Lord is ever wasted: "Know that in the Lord your labor is not in vain" (1 Cor 15:58). That heartening insight is further underscored by the stirring words of the author of the epistle to the Hebrews: "God is not unjust; he will not overlook your work and the love that you showed for his sake in serving the saints, as you still do" (Heb 6:10). To experience the enriching effect of these passages, however, you must really *trust* in them, just as you trust God for everything guaranteed by his holy Word. Trusting in those very promises is itself an act of virtue.

Trust is looking at a barren field, watered only by sweat and tears, and knowing that it will burst forth some day in a harvest of golden grain.

NINETY-NINE
Progress and Trust

A telephone was installed in the White House in 1870, but not on the president's desk. *For fifty-one years*, the presidents of the most advanced country in the world had to go out into the hall to use the single White House phone. The can opener was invented half a century after the tin can was invented. The neon sign was invented in France in 1910, but it wasn't known in America until 1923, when its first appearance stopped traffic in Los Angeles. Modern technology may be amazing, but at times its progress has been glacially slow.

We marvel at our awesomely rapid technological progress today, as we take for granted the availability of even handheld global-reaching mobile videophones that operate via satellite and were undreamed of only a few years ago. However, progress hasn't always been that brisk.

Like technology, our lives in general, and our spiritual growth in particular, may have spurts of progress with periods of stagnation, like sporadically congested freeway traffic. Yet we always expect to reach our destination, regardless of long or short periods of retardation in our progress.

Sometimes our progress seems to be retarded because our visibility is limited, when the Lord hides from us his long-range plans. It is especially at these interludes of confusion that our trust in his guidance is challenged. In air travel we trust the pilot or navigator to get us to our destination, even while we fly through blinding clouds or through the darkness of night. God is a very experienced pilot, and we have no choice but to trust him to make our progress sure, even if we have to fly through air turbulence while progressing.

At times, we ourselves are forced to navigate through unnerving situations, as when we drive a car through a fog bank. Our trust is even more challenged as a motorist in such a situation than as a passenger in a plane. The road signs are there, but can't be seen easily. When life's road signs are not easily visible in the fog, we must trust that the Lord will lift the fog in time for us to see the road signs that will direct us to what he wants us to do with our lives. As we keep moving forward, the signs will be seen more clearly, and we can then peer through the fog bank for the next road sign without anxiety.

Trust enables us to be lovingly and actively open to God in his constant, ever-loving desire to improve us, in and through all of life's vicissitudes. When we learn to trust we learn to accept ourselves as small acorns, knowing that we will grow. We must keep in mind that spiritual growth, even when it is slow, is still progress. We are tiny acorns that are designed by the Creator to survive drought and battering storms until we reach the full status of mighty oaks; in order to do so, all that is required is that we keep our ground—that is, stay rooted in Christ.

ONE HUNDRED
Direction and Trust

There's a cutesy axiom that says, "When you don't know which way to turn, follow God's directions: turn right!" It's not enough, though, just to turn right; we must also "keep to the right." That's the bottom-line description of character. Aristotle's definition of good character in his *Nicomachean Ethics* is living a life of *right* conduct in relation to oneself and to others. (As a pagan, he didn't spell out God's role in this schema.) Christian moralists like St. Thomas Aquinas later demonstrated how this proper relationship to oneself and to others actually embraces God as its substrate, as Jesus shows in his do-it-to-these-and-you-do-it-to-me norm (see Mt 25:40).

Aristotle's list of directions for character formation includes: 1) Moral *knowing* (judging what is right); 2) Moral *feeling* (desiring to do only right); and 3) Moral *doing* (acting on what is right). He expatiates each of these directions, and of course they have been further expounded upon in Christian writings through the centuries. Nevertheless, God's holy Word spells out each of these norms in even more ways and contexts.

An often-quoted quip says, "When all else fails, follow directions." When looking for directions, we Christians can't say we don't have a road map; we have the very best directions, handed down to us through philosophy, theology, and divine revelation. In trusting the reliability of road maps we implicitly trust the cartographers who have designed them. When we really come to rely on the Divine Cartographer, however, we won't need to wait until all else fails before following his directions. They lead right to the heart of God.

ONE HUNDRED ONE
Disappointment and Trust

I think it was Confucius who said, "Happiness does not consist in having what you want, but in wanting what you have."

One frequent cause of disappointment, especially in our prayers of petition, is that God does not give us what we want, but what we need. "Your heavenly Father knows that you need all these things" (Mt 6:32). In such a case, we are disappointed because our priorities may be misplaced and our value system inverted.

Occasionally we should ask ourselves what our priorities really are. To help us refocus, Jesus advises: "Strive first for the kingdom of God and his righteousness, and all these things will be given to you as well" (Mt 6:33). Attaining this holiness ("righteousness") should leave us immune to disappointment, because when we have God and his love (manifested by his beneficence toward us), we have everything we need, spiritually. The answers to our physical needs come as an unfailing bonus.

The Israelites, during the great exodus, yearning for the luxurious pots of meat they had enjoyed in Egypt (see Ex 16:3), were disappointed because only their needs and not their wants were fulfilled. Yet they were miraculously fed for forty years by the daily bread of heaven-sent manna and life-sustaining water from a rock (see Dt 8:15-16), along with honey and oil also from a rock (see Dt 32:13), and even their clothing was miraculous preserved for forty years in the desert environment (see Dt 8:4). These are the same three needs Jesus refers to in Matthew's gospel (6:31, 33): "Do not worry, saying 'What will we eat?' or 'What will we drink?' or 'What will we wear?...all these things will be given to you." If our spiritual aspirations are prioritized—seeking first holiness and the kingship of God—then all else will be provided; but we must continually seek first his kingdom and his righteousness.

Our spiritual needs come before, not instead of, our physical needs. Thus, really *trusting in God's promised provisions for our life-needs*, with spiritual goals at the top of our shopping list, will immunize us against any disappointment. When our wants are subordinate to our needs, especially our spiritual needs, the art of *trusting God without disappointment* is the inevitable result, and the reward that awaits us is equally inevitable. It is the one that Paul was allowed to preview: "No eye has seen, nor ear heard, nor the human heart conceived, what God has prepared for those who love him" (1 Cor 2:9).